THE PLAN TO WIN

A Step-by-Step System to Finally Achieve Your Goals

Spring Hempsey

Mindful Gnome Press

Published by Mindful Gnome Press LLC
Pasadena, California

The Plan to Win / Spring Hempsey. -- 1st ed.

Library of Congress Control Number: 2025927856

ISBN 979-8-9943185-0-8 (pbk)
ISBN 979-8-9943185-1-5 (eBook)

This book is dedicated to my students, past and present, who push me to think deeply, ask better questions, and improve my teaching. You show me where I can do better, which has led me to create clearer plans and stronger systems to help you succeed. Each year, I am reminded of how amazing you are, both inside and far beyond the classroom, and it remains one of my greatest privileges to have been part of your journey.

CONTENTS

*Success comes from designing systems that make the
right actions easier.*
—Katy Milkman

INTRODUCTION

We all have plans and dreams, but too few of us ever really pursue them.

Picture Lisa: a wife, a dog mom, and a full-time teacher, well known in her community for her spectacular annual Oscar party. She loves coming up with new themes, making the decorations, creating the invitations and ballots, and she even makes all the hors d'oeuvres herself. Every year, her party guests tell her she should start a catering or party-planning business, and she just smiles and says, "One day."

Secretly, she dreams of taking the leap. She has studied her local competitors and researched cottage food licensing rules for her city. Yet, for some reason, she hasn't made progress. She always talks about starting a business as if it's just a dream.

She's frustrated because she knows what she wants and is sure it would bring a significant positive change in her life. However, she can't seem to stick with it long enough to make any headway. She makes to-do lists, but they never really get her anywhere. She gets caught up in crises at work or home, and just hasn't gotten around to planning how to make her dream come true.

This is where the pattern can change.

The problem Lisa has, and maybe you do too, isn't that she lacks motivation, intelligence, or determination; it's that most goal-setting and planning systems collapse when real life shows up. You hype yourself up, start working toward your goal, sure that this time you'll make it happen, and when something interferes with your routine, you get distracted and put your dream aside. For some people, that dream gets sidelined forever.

Most people don't fail because they lack motivation. They fail because motivation isn't consistent or reliable; it fails them when life gets complicated, and life is always complicated.

For most people, it's easy to get overwhelmed by competing priorities, limited energy, and the constant pressure to "do more," especially when you don't have a method for dealing with them.

Working harder doesn't work. It won't get you what you want because:

- Success requires better decision-making, not greater effort.
- Motivation is unreliable when your energy is limited or depleted.
- Willpower always fails when you're stressed; that's normal.

And I can prove it. Using stories about people such as cosmetics maven Mary Kay Ash, football coach Bill Walsh, *Little House on the Prairie* author Laura Ingalls Wilder, and even Martha Stewart, I'll show you that successful people don't work harder; they plan better. And because of that better plan, when things go sideways and crises arise, they handle them effectively, since their plan has contingencies in place. They were ready, so they weren't pushed off course. And they knew that even when they moved slowly toward their goal, they were still moving. Because real life and the PLAN to WIN are about progress, not perfection.

The Importance of Planning

Some people mistakenly assume that planning is time-consuming, so they avoid it or rush ahead without strategizing how they'll reach their goal. That approach will take up much more of your time in the long run and be much less efficient than planning where you're headed and how you'll get there in advance. A little bit of planning can save hours of confusion, decision-making stress, and the need to backtrack or redo.

Brian Tracy, author of *Eat That Frog*, wrote that ten to twelve minutes of planning saves two hours of work.[1] And often attributed to Abraham Lincoln is the saying, "Give me six hours to chop down a tree, and I will spend the first four sharpening the axe," demonstrating the time-honored belief in the importance of planning and preparation before starting a goal. The main takeaway here is that taking the time to prepare, such as sharpening the axe, greatly improves efficiency and effectiveness, leading to faster, higher-quality results when it's time to take action, like chopping the tree.

Taking the time to plan also lessens the need for motivation. A plan helps you build momentum, so when you lack motivation or things feel difficult, you have something else to push you forward. Not that everything will be hard; it won't. There will be easy parts, too. And it's important to remember that you've done hard things all your life, so you can certainly do this.

Where Most People Get Stuck

Most planning systems do one of two things: inspire you (motivation, hype, big dreams) or overwhelm you (checklists, productivity hacks, rigid timelines). However, they aren't solutions, they're just bandages. Armed with temporary motivation, you may feel a surge of confidence that this attempt will be the one that works. Or you might buy a new device that blocks access to social media, which can help you stay on top of your priorities. But it is likely that you'll get frustrated with the complexity of the new productivity tools you invested in, and unfortunately, if you continue to approach your situation without a proven system for processing all your must-dos, your motivation will quickly wane.

A core problem many ambitious people face isn't knowing what they want, but struggling to translate that clarity into consistent progress. Fortunately, the book you're currently reading introduces a practical, research-informed planning system designed around how adults actually learn, change, and follow through. It can help you move from scattered effort to focused execution—without burnout or having to start over every few months.

My Classroom Experience

I know this to be true because, pre-PLAN to WIN, I experienced it first-hand. Early in my career, I was overwhelmed by everything required in teaching AP US History. My solution was to create a system that would make it easier for me and ensure consistent success for my students on their end-of-year AP exam. So, one summer, I started mapping out how I could transform this class. In June, I was totally committed and working on my plan. By July, I was getting distracted by various summer events, and by early August, I had decided this wasn't the year to roll out a new class.

The problem wasn't my idea, my plan for redesigning the class, or even how I was going to make it happen. My problem back then was that I quickly got overwhelmed by everything that had to be done, and when distractions arose, I didn't know how to take small steps toward progress. I had an all-or-nothing mindset, and without a plan, I burned out from decision fatigue when inevitable distractions arose. Many times, I felt like I was making no progress, which was demotivating. The reality was that I didn't have a *plan*; I had a *to-do list* with no real deadline. And that's typically how planning guides work—they help you break down tasks and encourage you to start doing stuff, but they don't necessarily provide guidance for the order you should do the tasks, and tend not to offer a schedule or base it on when you need to be finished.

That's why I didn't accomplish my goal that year. I set a goal, broke it down into tasks, and then got overwhelmed. Instead of having a plan each day when I walked into my classroom, I planned the lesson for each day the night before and didn't really connect those day-to-day plans to the year-long goal I had envisioned. The students made some progress in their learning, but I knew I could do better, for me and for them, and that it didn't have to be this overwhelming. This was the catalyst for creating the PLAN to WIN system.

What I lacked then and what the PLAN to WIN offers is:

- Step-by-step guidance on how to break goals down until they are manageable
- Support in zeroing in on the one goal that will impact most of the others
- Help in determining how much work it will really take to successfully achieve your goal
- A schedule to keep you moving forward
- Confidence that you are capable of making your goal a reality
- An approach to navigate setbacks without quitting
- Accounting for real constraints (work, family, health, energy)

You don't need new goals. You need a way to move forward without starting over every time something goes wrong or you get stuck.

I know this because I have spent a lot of time learning how behavior change really works. I researched why motivated, capable people often struggle to reach their goals, and how decision fatigue can undermine even the best of intentions. I read stories, took courses, and joined programs, then applied what I learned to my own life, which ultimately benefited my students. This process not only helped me see what was holding me back but also taught me how to overcome obstacles and make progress more effectively and consistently.

What Successful People Do Differently

The PLAN to WIN framework is a step-by-step system for setting a year-long goal and pursuing it. It's not about manifesting your desires out of thin air or finding a shortcut to achieving a dream outcome. Instead, it's a methodical process that breaks down your big goal into bite-sized tasks that you put on your schedule and do. Some people make it to that last step, of putting an action item on their calendar, and then they simply don't complete it. Rather than do what they know they need to, they choose to stay where they are and not invite change.

But even more people never even finish their plan. Sure, they envision it, they imagine what their life could be like with this goal attained, they may even start to think about what, exactly, it would take for them to get where they want to go. This is where so many people stop. They make a list of steps, check it twice, and file it away. And it ends there—some realizing they're not done planning and others under the mistaken impression that identifying the steps required to reach their goal is enough. But it's really just the beginning of the process.

Entrepreneurs are known to do this, actually. They spend time, energy, and money developing a comprehensive plan for their business. They map out what they're going to offer customers, how they'll deliver it, what kind of staff they'll need, how they'll market their company, and how they'll successfully manage cash flow challenges early on. They may even present it to banks to line up start-up capital. The biggest problem is what happens next: They file that plan away on their shelves or in a desk drawer. Instead of using it to manage their daily activities, they push it aside and all but forget about it. This is where the PLAN to WIN can come in—but it will only deliver the best results when it becomes a consistent part of your daily process.

Most goal-achievement systems still treat success as a willpower or productivity problem when in reality it is a learning and behavior-change problem. A successful planning process, which I define as a clear, step-by-step program that enables you to take the measures you need and then do them, does eventually require action. But you need a process to follow, first and foremost.

I see this firsthand in my classroom when students transfer in from other schools and immediately struggle—not that all new students struggle, but some do. They want to do well in my class, are motivated, and have a track record of success that demonstrates their capability. But when we dig into what's keeping them from the grades they're used to, it often becomes clear that their study habits are failing them. Or that their old way of studying isn't working anymore because they have a lot more homework to contend with.

The solution? A new process, based on their current reality and what it's going to take to be successful. That's exactly what you're going to learn in the coming pages.

THE PLAN TO WIN

Picturing Success

Picturing Success has you visualizing what you want your life to look like, then zeroing in on what you want to have happen to design your ideal life.

Lock in a Goal

Lock in a Goal helps guide you from the big picture to a clear understanding of the specific goal you want to achieve over the next 365 days. This will help you narrow your focus down to a specific, measurable goal.

Analyze Your Starting Point

Analyze your Starting Point helps you take stock of where you are now in relation to your desired outcome. You're effectively getting clear about the gap between where you are and where you want to be, so you can close it as quickly as possible.

Name the Elements

Name the Elements is where you'll identify the key components you'll need to take to reach your goal. You'll list all of these out, in no particular order.

Write the Order Out

Write the Order Out is where you'll organize your list and put your tasks into a logical sequence.

Implement the Plan

Implement the Plan is where you go from planning to action, taking the first step toward your goal.

Navigate Challenges

Navigate Challenges has you identifying potential obstacles to your success and developing solutions to overcome them.

What Makes the PLAN to WIN Unique

The PLAN to WIN is unique because it applies principles from learning science and behavior change research to goal achievement. It shows you how to design goals, plans, and actions that stick. When progress is structured the way learning works, consistency becomes sustainable, and long-term success becomes far more achievable.

This book walks you through the entire process step by step. Each chapter builds on the last, while working at your own pace. The PLAN to WIN is also repeatable with any new goal you want to set. When I use the word "win," I'm referring to the successful achievement of your goal, whatever that is. Your win could be something practical, like paying down your credit card debt or finding a new apartment. Or it could be loftier, like getting into graduate school or mapping out a way to reach your retirement savings goal.

This book isn't one you finish, forget, and put on your bookshelf. It's a system or framework you can return to whenever life changes, or you're inspired to make a change. You can start where you are, move at whatever pace you're most comfortable, and adjust as needed. You can even pivot if need be; it's flexible.

By the end of this book, you will be able to take any personal or professional goal and turn it into a clear, step-by-step plan that you can execute with confidence.

In chapters 1–7, you'll learn how to visualize your ideal life, choose the one goal that is going to make the biggest difference, determine how to go from where you are to where you want to be, break down all of the required activities, organize them, and then schedule them. You'll also pick up some tips for dealing with inevitable bumps in the road that will attempt to derail you, so that you can stay on course.

In these seven chapters, you'll not only learn about each step of the process, but you'll also learn *why* these steps matter, through relevant research that explains how it supports the system as a whole. You'll also see the step in action through stories you can relate to—

examples from well-known achievers, moments from my own classroom, and Lisa's ongoing journey from idea to action.

From there, each step is broken down into smaller, practical components, with clear explanations, examples, and guiding questions to help you apply the process directly to your own goals. Every chapter concludes with a concise **Chapter Cheat Sheet** that distills the step into its essential actions and questions. Because PLAN to WIN is designed to be used again and again for different goals, these cheat sheets allow you to move quickly through future plans—without re-reading material you already know—so you can focus on what matters most: taking intentional, effective action.

In the last four chapters, I'll walk you through four case studies of how I approached my goals using this system, so you can see how to apply it to your life.

Here is how the book is organized to lead you through each step of the process:

- **Chapter 1: P—Picture Your Success** has you visualizing what you want your life to look like, then zeroing in on what you want to happen to design your ideal life.
- **Chapter 2: L—Lock In On One Goal** helps guide you from the big picture to a clear understanding of the specific goal you want to achieve over the next 365 days. This will help you narrow your focus down to a specific, measurable objective.
- **Chapter 3: A—Analyze Your Starting Point** helps you take stock of where you are now in relation to your desired outcome. You're effectively getting clear about the gap between where you are and where you want to be, so you can close it as quickly as possible.
- **Chapter 4: N—Name the Elements** will help you identify the key components you'll need to take to reach your goal. You'll list all of these out, in no particular order.

- **Chapter 5: W—Write It Out** is where you'll organize your list and put your tasks into a logical sequence.
- **Chapter 6: I—Implement the Plan** is where you go from planning to action, taking the first step toward your goal.
- **Chapter 7: N—Navigate Challenges** has you identifying potential obstacles to your success and developing solutions to overcome them.
- **Chapters 8–11** are four case studies that show what it looks like to PLAN to WIN for four very common goals: starting a business, losing weight, writing a book, and creating an online course.

Between the chapters of the book, you'll also find sections called **Mentor Notes & Insights**. These are separate from the PLAN to WIN steps; think of them as the advice of a wise mentor. These sections offer observations, research, and experience on learning, changing behavior, and achieving goals. Their purpose is to add context, not complicate things. You can choose to read only the ones of interest to you, and you can read them in any order. Some may resonate now, while others might be relevant later—or not at all. *They provide insight into the thinking, research, and lived experience that informed this system, offering perspectives and tools you may find useful along the way, but they are not required to complete the system or achieve your goal.*

The PLAN to WIN is practical, pressure-tested, and built for smart, competent people who are tired of starting over. This approach is a way to move forward, not by doing more, but by doing the right things in the right order.

After you read The PLAN to WIN, you won't have to wonder how to approach reaching your goal because the self-guided system will tell you exactly what you need to do next.

Every meaningful transformation is simply:

Picture → Lock In → Analyze → Name → Write → Implement → Navigate

That is how you win.

Let's get started!

Create the highest, grandest vision possible for your life, because you become what you believe.
—Oprah Winfrey

CHAPTER ONE

P—PICTURE YOUR SUCCESS

Olympic swimmer Michael Phelps has talked repeatedly about the various ways he pictures his success—using visualization techniques to win races. He credits this practice with helping him achieve his goals, including winning an Olympic medal.

At age eleven, Phelps's coach, Bob Bowman, gave his mother a book on relaxation techniques, which she began using with her son. Every night, he would practice relaxing each of his muscles, then imagine himself in the pool. Recognizing that he was mentally rehearsing for upcoming races, Phelps routinely worked through visualizations of all kinds of scenarios, from crises such as tearing his suit to his goggles filling with water, which actually happened at the 2008 Olympics.

Because Phelps had run through the possibility of his goggles failing, he was mentally and physically prepared to proceed as if nothing had happened. Although he couldn't see where he was going at all in the water, he counted his strokes to gauge how many strokes he was from the pool wall—and still won gold.

Phelps had pictured success—winning the race no matter what obstacle appeared in his way—and achieved his goal. Between 2000 and 2016, Phelps competed in five Olympic Games and collected twenty-eight medals, twenty-three of which are gold. He pictured his desired result and attained it. Now it's your turn.

Chapter Objective: By the end of this chapter, you will be able to **Picture** your success and describe what it looks like using all five senses.

Developing a Visualization Muscle

Visualization is a widely accepted technique for improving the odds of success, and there are numerous stories of successful people using it. Football star Tom Brady used visualization to run through different on-field scenarios to prepare for his games. Early in his career, actor Jim Carrey wrote himself a $10 million check, which he kept in his wallet, to prepare for the day he could cash it; his movie *Dumb and Dumber*, with a $10 million fee, made that possible. Spanx founder Sara Blakely used visualization for fifteen years to prepare for a guest appearance on The Oprah Winfrey Show. And Oprah herself has long been a champion of visualization for goal achievement.

While visualization is a proven tool for achieving goals, what to visualize and how to visualize it are often debated. Experts agree, however, that it's not a one-time event. You can't just picture winning your local 5K race or buying your dream car once, then never think about it again and hope you'll be successful. You need to visualize your desired outcome routinely.

You don't have to do it every day (though you could), but you do need to reflect on it often enough to keep the vision alive in your mind. You could pick a time of day or a situation when you'll visualize your desired outcome, so you repeatedly return to it and build it into a mental muscle.

For example, you could decide that every Friday after work is a great time to practice visualization as you start to wind down your workweek and relax. Or maybe you decide that every time you drive a parent to a doctor's appointment, you'll use your waiting time in the doctor's office to visualize success. Or you could make it part of your daily routine and use the time after you put dinner in the oven to visualize reaching your goal.

You'll have the best chance of achieving your goal if you start with visualization. Picturing what success will look like helps your brain identify pathways to get you there. At this stage, it doesn't matter what your goal is or why your goal is important to you—just imagine what it will look and feel like when you accomplish it, and your odds will increase dramatically.

The Power of Visualization

Plenty of research has confirmed the power of visualizing success, especially in sports. One of the earlier studies was conducted in 1967 by Australian psychologist Alan Richardson[1], who examined the effects of visualization on sports performance. He divided his participants into three groups. The first group was told to report back in thirty days; they made no changes to their lifestyle. The second group was told to practice making basketball free throws at the gym for twenty minutes a day for the next thirty days. And the third group was told to visualize making free throws for twenty minutes every day; they couldn't touch a basketball, only imagine the shots going in.

As expected, the first group, the control, showed no improvement in their free-throw abilities. The second group improved by 24 percent through practice. Surprisingly, the third group improved nearly as much, increasing their free-throw skills by 23 percent through visualization alone.

More recently, in 2016, researchers Blankert and Hamstra of Maastricht University in the Netherlands confirmed this success by using a visualization technique called PETTLEP (**P**hysical, **E**nvironment, **T**ask, **T**iming, **L**earning, **E**motion, and **P**erspective) with tennis. Sixty-five tennis players were asked to serve twenty times and then participate in a PETTLEP visualization exercise. The players were divided into three groups: One group visualized improved serves, another visualized serving better than their opponents, and a third group visualized both. Everyone then hit twenty more serves. Of the three groups, the one that visualized both improved serves and better performance had superior outcomes, missing fewer serves and hitting the service box more frequently. Visualizing success significantly improved their performance.[2]

The fact is that visualization alters your brain's pathways and forges new neural connections, both of which are beneficial in achieving the desired outcome. Visualization primes your brain for success. That's the true power of picturing your success.

My Classroom Experience

Picturing success, for me, was not an abstract outcome or a test score on a spreadsheet—it was a felt experience. I pictured walking into my classroom without the constant low-level panic that comes from trying to teach an impossible amount of content. I could see a clean, intentional plan in front of me, not a cluttered to-do list. I could hear a more focused discussion and fewer frantic questions about what mattered most. I could feel the difference in my body—less tension in my shoulders, more energy at the end of the day—because I wasn't making dozens of instructional decisions on the fly. I imagined the quiet confidence that comes from knowing the system is doing the work, guiding both my teaching and my students' learning toward the same outcome. And I pictured the ultimate proof: more students walking into the AP exam prepared, steady, and capable because the year had been designed to get them there.

Like many teachers, I use Backward Design in course planning, a framework developed by Grant Wiggins and Jay McTighe in their book *Understanding by Design*. Backward Design starts with teachers identifying the desired learning outcomes to plan their curriculum, instruction, and assessments effectively.

As a teacher, my classroom planning always starts with picturing where I want my students to end up. I visualize the outcome I want for them: a 3 or higher on the AP exam. Imagine a teacher showing up every day without knowing what they wanted their students to learn and do by the end of the day, week, month, or year? Teachers must have clear learning goals for their students and create daily, weekly, quarterly, and yearly plans to ensure that their students achieve the year's learning and are prepared to move on to the next grade or level.

For personal and professional goals, this step is even more critical since it isn't something adults regularly think about or break down in their lives. If you don't know where you want to end up, you probably won't know when you get there.

Lisa's Journey

For Lisa, the aspiring caterer, success meant more than just starting a business. It was a vision of a better life. She saw herself on a Saturday morning in her kitchen, calm and unhurried. She was preparing for a paid event she was excited about. She imagined the sounds of conversation at a party she had planned. It made her feel proud to hand someone an invoice for her work. She felt the relief of owning something that fit into her life. Most importantly, she pictured the quiet confidence from making her dreams real—proof that she had turned her ideas into something tangible.

Picturing a New Life, Post-Crisis

Martha Stewart doesn't often talk directly about visualization. Still, she is a consummate planner, which partly explains how she has been able to remake her entire career and build a media empire, even after a stint in prison that could have derailed her brand.

Stewart's career as a lifestyle mogul started with a home renovation. During the many months she worked to update and upgrade the home she and her then-husband had purchased, she immersed herself in mastering French cooking, thanks to Julia Child's cookbook, and launched a catering business with a friend. After catering a business party for her husband, she caught the eye of a publisher, who hired her to write and publish her first book, *Entertaining*, in 1982. The book became a bestseller and laid the groundwork for Stewart's bigger vision to come to fruition.

Based on the success of that first book, Stewart convinced Time Warner to launch the magazine Martha Stewart Living, in 1990.[3] In 1993, she launched a syndicated TV show by the same name. Then, in 1997, she purchased the magazine and TV show from Time Warner and established Martha Stewart Omnimedia, which went public two years later, making her a billionaire.

After being found guilty of insider trading in 2004, she was sent to prison, a sentence that could have led to the collapse of her empire. But it didn't, because Stewart was committed to rebuilding rather than retreating. According to her recent Netflix documentary, Martha pictured her comeback while she was in prison. She "contemplated the future," rather than focusing on the past. She continued to plan, "new ideas germinating," looking ahead to being productive again. She was picturing what she wanted her life after release to look like, and she used that vision to shape her comeback, which, by all accounts, has been successful.

The PLAN to WIN in Action

Picturing your success is the first step in the PLAN to WIN system and is an integral part of the planning process. To begin, you have to decide what your result will look like. What will be different in your life? How will you be different personally or professionally?

When picturing your success, start by dreaming big, then slowly narrow your focus.

Let me walk you through what this looks like. Don't hold back, dream big!

Step 1: Clarify Your Big-Picture Life Direction

Your first step is to think about where you want your life to be in the long term, more than twenty years from now. What do you want to be, do, or have by the time you retire or on your ninetieth birthday, for example? What would make you feel proud? What would give your life meaning and worth? Describe that. Get clear about it.

Create a picture in your head of what that moment looks like. Picture all five senses. What does that success look like? What does it feel like physically? Are there smells or tastes associated with this success? What sounds are you hearing around you as you celebrate this moment? What emotions are present?

Step 2: Describe the Bridge Between Now and That Future

Now that you know where you're heading in your life long-term, narrow your scope to the next ten years. At the end of ten years, what do you want to have accomplished? What will your life look like at that point? Who is in it? How do you spend your time?

Then reflect on your current life path. What are you willing and not willing to change in your life to achieve that ten-year vision? In life, there are often trade-offs. To do X, you may have to give up on Y. For example, accepting a job overseas means you cannot remain in your hometown. Relatedly, are there things you may regret not doing?

Now, work backward from ten years to five years. For your ten-year vision to be realized, what must be in place by the five-year point? What skills or experience will you need to have gained by year five?

If your goal in ten years is to be a professor at an Ivy League university and you're currently in a PhD program, where will you need to be in five years to be on course to land a tenure-track position at an exclusive school? Will you need to have graduated? Published a paper or two? Attended conferences to start building a network of colleagues in academia?

Step 3: Identify What Success Looks Like One Year from Today

Narrowing your focus further, let's look at next year. If you only achieved one major thing this year, what would move you closer to your long-term future? Think of all the possible answers to this question. You don't need to decide on a goal just yet; you're exploring the possibilities.

If you aspire to become an adoptive parent in five years, what could you do in the next year to position yourself for success? What actions will move the needle for you?

As you explore what goal you might want to focus on for the next year, ask yourself what you need to know to make sure the goal truly supports your long-term dreams. How do these one-year goal ideas support your big-picture life direction? Talking through your perspective and thought process with others can help clarify your plans and your dreams.

Chapter Cheat Sheet

Step 1: Clarify Your Big-Picture Life Direction
- What would make your life feel more meaningful and worth-while?
- What do you want to be, do, or have by the time you retire or on your 90th birthday?

Step 2: Describe the Bridge Between Now and That Future
- At the end of ten years, what do you want to have accomplished?

- If your ten-year vision is to be realized, what must be in place by the five-year point?

Step 3: Identify What Success Looks Like One Year from Today

- What are some things you could accomplish this year that would move you closer to your long-term picture of success?
- How do these one-year goal ideas support your big-picture life direction?

Mentor Notes & Insights

Setting Boundaries

As you work on your plan and move toward your goal, you'll need to say "no" to things that might distract you. Setting these boundaries is key to achieving your goal, even if it's new or a little uncomfortable at first. It is worth it in the long run.

It's okay to put yourself first. You can take time for yourself without feeling guilty. And remember: Saying "no" can mean "not right now," rather than "never." That difference matters.

For example, if your neighbor invites you for coffee while you're heading for a walk, invite them to join you or suggest catching up later. You're not rejecting them; it's just not a good time.

Use this method when starting or during important tasks. If you're writing, ask someone to talk later, after you finish for the day. The same applies to cooking or reviewing finances. Don't let others distract you from your goals. Just ask to reconnect another time.

Saying "no" can be hard. It's easy to put things off and think you'll resume later, but that's not always realistic. Getting sidetracked can lead to losing focus.

Think of your commitments like appointments. If you were at your doctor's office, you wouldn't take calls or respond to messages during your appointment. You'd give the doctor your full attention. Do the same for your own commitments.

Setting boundaries isn't easy, but it's essential for making time for your goals.

If you schedule time for activities like painting or practicing an instrument, protect that time. Don't let others interrupt or change your plans. Be as dedicated to your schedule as you would be during an important appointment. To reduce distractions, turn off your phone, silence notifications, and put a note on your door if needed. This signals to others that you're busy.

On a plane, flight attendants tell you to put on your own oxygen mask before helping others. This isn't selfish; it's necessary. You must take care of yourself first to help others. If you don't, you won't be able to assist anyone.

You can't make progress if every little thing distracts you. Most things aren't real emergencies and can wait. Sometimes, you need to say "no" and focus on your own goals.

CHAPTER 2

L-LOCK IN ON ONE GOAL

As a child, Laura Ingalls Wilder and her family moved regularly across the Midwest in pursuit of a better life. Throughout her life, she became a farmer, a teacher, a dressmaker, and eventually, a wife and mother.

When she and her husband lost all their savings in the stock market crash of 1929[1], Laura needed to find a way to make a living. Her daughter Rose, a writer herself, encouraged her mother to write a book about her childhood. This became Laura's singular strategy for survival.

With her daughter's encouragement, Laura locked in on one clear goal and wrote *Little House in the Big Woods*, which offered a young child's perspective on a year of frontier living. This singular focus, combined with Rose's industry connections, allowed Laura, at age sixty-five, to have her work published by Harper & Brothers. It went on to sell more than sixty million copies. The success of that first book led her to add seven more titles by 1943, but she began with one book as her initial goal. That focus on one goal led to her success. This chapter will show you how to do the same.

Chapter Objective: By the end of this chapter, you will create a list of possible one-year goals that support the picture of your future success. Choose the one you will focus on first, and turn it into a clear SMART goal (Specific, Measurable, Achievable, Relevant, Time-bound) with a statement that reminds you of how this goal supports your big dreams.

Locking in on One Goal

People set goals for every aspect of their lives. Some of the most common include losing weight or improving health, saving money, or paying off a debt. But goals can also involve completing a creative project, such as writing a book or painting a canvas, or training for a physical competition, such as an Ironman or a marathon. Other popular goals include learning a new skill, like playing an instrument or knitting; starting a side business; launching an online course; or changing careers. And sometimes goals involve strengthening mental and emotional skills, such as setting boundaries or reducing stress.

Unfortunately, many people never make progress toward their goals because the goals are too general, such as "get healthy." Or they have so many different goals that they spread their efforts out and fail to make headway on any of them. In trying to accomplish too much at once, they end up accomplishing nothing. The reason we're selecting one goal is to help you focus your time, energy, and money on planning and achieving it.

A colleague of mine frequently complains about not having enough money. I'm not sure why that is, exactly. It's unclear whether they don't earn enough to cover their expenses or if they spend too much on non-essentials. Either way, their goal for some time has been "to get ahead."

To me, that goal is too general. What exactly does "ahead" look like? So, I gently pushed them to define what that would look like. "Being able to pay all their bills and have a little left over" was what they told me. That sounded reasonable, so I suggested they take the advice of a well-known personal finance guru and aim for one goal: Set aside $1,000 in an emergency fund by the end of the year.

Although they initially argued that saving $1,000 wasn't enough to fix all their issues, I pointed out that it would be a step toward building a financial cushion. It was one specific, measurable, achievable, reasonable, and time-bound goal that they could aim for and know when they had reached it. That seemed to make sense, and for a while, I didn't hear any more complaints about being broke. Then, a few months later, they proudly told me they had saved $1,000. They were now focused on paying off a credit card; setting that first goal gave them the momentum to turn things around. You can do this, too. You just need to set one goal.

Starting with your "Picture of Success" from chapter 1, you now need to **Lock in** on one specific goal before you start planning. Science has shown that people who lock in a goal and plan it out are more likely to achieve it. A big reason for this higher level of success is that you are spending intentional time thinking through what you want to accomplish and how you want to accomplish it by considering how it connects to and supports the larger vision you have for your life.

One of the biggest challenges in planning your big goals is figuring out which goal to start with—which one to plan first. Many people become paralyzed by indecision, unsure of which one to start with or where to begin. That's most likely because, as humans, we naturally have multiple goals, often for different aspects of our lives.

You may want to earn a promotion at work, find a life partner, go on a long or difficult hike, lose twenty pounds, or earn an advanced degree, to name a few possibilities. None of these goals is mutually exclusive, which can make choosing only one to start with difficult.

Do you begin with the one you think will be easiest to accomplish? Or do you choose the one that will have the most significant impact on your quality of life? Or something else?

The good news is that you can do all of them, and more, in due time. But you can't plan them out simultaneously. Once you have your goal planned, you might be able to pursue more than one, but successful planning is a one-at-a-time process.

If you're having difficulty deciding which of the goals you want to focus on first, Gary Keller, author of *The ONE Thing*, wrote a whole book about the importance of focusing on one goal at a time, suggesting that the fundamental question you need to start with is: "What's the ONE thing I can do such that by doing it, everything else will be easier or unnecessary?"[2] Try asking yourself that question and see which of the goals you have in mind seems to be the answer.

Researchers Joshua S. Rubinstein, David E. Meyer, and Jeffrey E. Evans state that, "Trying to do multiple things at once can decrease productivity by up to 40 percent."[3] Their research examines the downsides of multitasking in general, but it holds true when applied to planning. Do one thing at a time for the best results.

Bestselling author James Clear, who wrote *Atomic Habits*, emphasized the importance of a singular focus when changing habits, noting that it helps you gain clarity on how to take action. Clear states, "Research has shown that you are 2x to 3x more likely to stick with your habits if you make a specific plan for when, where, and how you will perform the behavior."[4] Those outlines for when, where, and how you will implement your plan are called *implementation intentions*. Clear further states that "follow-up research has discovered implementation intentions only work when you focus on one thing at a time." That solitary focus on one goal dramatically improves your chances of achieving it.

My Classroom Experience

My first goal was to create a repeatable planning system for teaching AP US History. This system should help me avoid feeling overwhelmed while boosting student success on the AP exam. I could measure this goal by tracking student performance, writing quality, and exam pass rates to see if it worked. It was achievable too; I wasn't changing the curriculum or the students, just how I planned and structured the year. The goal was relevant since reducing my stress and improving student outcomes were linked—both were essential for long-term success. Plus, it was time-bound, meaning the system had to be effective within one academic year and lead to strong results on the AP exam each May. By locking in this goal, I turned planning from a guessing game into a clear, evidence-based process.

Lisa's Journey

Once Lisa could see the outcome, she was able to set a clear goal. She went from a general goal of starting a business to a more specific one: launching a local party-planning and catering business within a year. This included getting her cottage food license and booking at least three paid events. Her goal had clear steps she could track. It fit her schedule, matched her desires, and had a deadline. By setting this goal, Lisa turned her dream into a plan, rather than something she might do someday.

Locking in on One Goal Gives Rise to a Multimillion-Dollar Business

Designer Vera Wang got her start in fashion as an editor at *Vogue* magazine, where she rose through the ranks for seventeen years. However, after not being chosen as editor-in-chief, she pivoted, going all-in on fashion design. Rather than continuing to climb someone else's career ladder, she decided to build her own, starting by taking a design role at Ralph Lauren in 1987.[5]

She was learning the ropes when she recognized a gap in the wedding dress market. After looking unsuccessfully for herself and realizing that her vision of a modern gown didn't yet exist, she designed her own, commissioning a dressmaker to sew it for $10,000.[6]

She launched the Vera Wang brand in 1990, focusing solely on modern, sophisticated wedding dress designs. She didn't try to launch a full clothing line; instead, she focused on wedding attire.

Vera opened her own storefront on Madison Avenue, down the street from her old *Vogue* office, and brought in high-end gowns from established designers to attract buyers while she was still unknown. Once the store was stocked, she turned to her former colleagues at *Vogue* and asked for coverage of her new business. And she got it: six whole pages. Future brides came running.

By 1992, she felt she knew enough about the market to launch her own line of wedding dresses, in two tiers: ready-to-wear and bespoke. She was successful by locking in on one goal and pursuing it doggedly for several years, ultimately building a company valued at over $700 million.[7]

The PLAN to WIN in Action

Locking in on a goal can be tricky, and clearly defining it requires skillful attention to detail, so let me walk you through the steps.

Step 1: Choose the ONE Primary Goal that Will Move You Closer to Your Envisioned Life

Go back to your one-year "Picture of Success" and all the potential goals you listed. Go through and label them as either big, medium, or small goals, based on the time you'll need to complete them. A big goal will take about twelve months to accomplish; a medium goal will take three to six months; and a small goal will take less than three months. A big goal might be something like writing a book or losing more than fifty pounds.

This system is designed to plan big goals, but once you've gone through the process of doing this, you can easily adapt this system to plan your medium and small goals.

Now that you've identified your big goal possibilities, the key is to prioritize and choose just one. In some cases, it will be clear which goal is your highest priority because you can see that it will have a positive impact on all your other aspirations. If you can tell right away, pick that one and get started planning it.

There might be clues about which goal to plan first. Maybe you're looking at your master list, and one will stand out as the most fun or the most rewarding, or maybe it actually has a deadline. If so, do that one first, because you're more likely to stick with it. However, the items on most people's lists have an arbitrary deadline. You want to start a business someday, or start a podcast, or learn how to draw. These are things you have thought about, but you haven't yet sat down to try to figure out the steps required to get them done.

But sometimes there isn't a clear, obvious standout. And in those cases, you might just need to choose one. Don't let yourself get paralyzed with indecision. Some people worry so much about choosing the wrong goal to start with that they never get anything done. It's called *analysis paralysis*. They're so caught up in choosing that they don't ever move forward. Sometimes you just have to pick one and get started, because that small action actually builds momentum.

When given a choice, concentrate on a goal that requires low effort and yields a high value or payoff first. For example, if your goal is to reduce your monthly expenses and you own a car, one small tactic could be to take the six-hour Automobile Association of America (AAA) defensive driving course.[8] The costs and benefits vary by state, but in California, you can pay around $39 and possibly save 10 percent right off the top of your insurance bill.

Finally, if you have twenty things on your master list, but you can only accomplish one of them this year, ask yourself which one is going to significantly make your life better next year? Which goal on your list will move you closer to that bigger, long-term vision you have? That's what it comes down to—and that's how you pick which one to plan first.

SMART GOAL

A goal is specific if it is clear, well-defined, detailed, and descriptive.

Express your goal in a way that makes it possible to measure whether you've been successful. In many cases, that requires converting a qualitative goal into a quantitative one or turning a description into a number.

Achievable goals are stretch goals— challenging but not out of reach.

Relevance refers to the impact reaching your goal will have on your life and the extent to which it reflects your values.

Time-bound means that you pick a due date to create a sense of urgency and focus. ut of reach.

Step 2: Turn Your Goal into a SMART Goal (Specific, Measurable, Achievable, Relevant, Time-bound)

Once you've decided which goal to plan first, it's helpful to write it out as a SMART goal. SMART goals are: Specific, Measurable, Achievable, Relevant, and Time-bound. This is not a new concept, and I'm not claiming to be its originator, but I do think it's a valuable approach to planning out what you want to accomplish. It's important to note that while tools like SMART goals can be effective, they often fail when used as a standalone solution. The PLAN to WIN's power lies in its full sequence, and setting a SMART goal is just a part of that sequence. Setting a clear, specific, and measurable goal helps ensure you can tell whether you've achieved it.

Specific

A goal is specific if it is clear, well-defined, detailed, and descriptive. Goals that are too broad or undefined would include statements like "lose weight," "get a raise at work," "travel more," or "attract more business." The problem is that because there are multiple ways to interpret and reach those goals, it's hard to know what success looks like. If you lose one pound, have you reached your goal? If you get the same 3 percent annual raise you've received for the last five years, did you accomplish your goal?

The difficulty with these examples is a lack of specificity. These goals are too broad, too generic, too vague. Specific goals use precise language, like "lose fifteen pounds," "earn a 10 percent raise at work," "take a two-week trip to Aruba," or "land $20,000 in new contracts for work."

Measurable

Expressing your goals in a way that makes it possible to measure whether you've been successful is another element of successful planning. In many cases, that requires converting a qualitative goal into a quantitative one or turning a description into a number. That's like transforming the goal of "exercise more" into "exercise at least three times a week for thirty minutes each." That's measurable. You can immediately determine if you've succeeded by tracking your numbers.

With measurable goals, you can tell if you're making progress, even if you haven't yet reached your stated objective.

If you're trying to save $6,000 next year, or $500/month, you can break that number down even further, to $125/week or, on average, $16.67/day. You can set daily and weekly goals and then compare the amount you save at regular intervals to see if you're behind or ahead of your target at any point in time.

For each measurable goal, try to list three to five milestones (smaller measurements) that will provide evidence that your plan is working. What milestones can you track that you'll be proud of?

If you've decided to run a 5K race in ninety days, you can set interim goals, or signals, to measure how close you're getting to your goal. In this case, you could track how many minutes you spend running each week in total; how far you run distance-wise; how you feel after each run, on a five-point scale; or how far you can run in a set amount of time, such as in thirty minutes.

Be sure that what you're measuring is related to your ultimate success. If you're training to run a race, measuring how much protein you eat daily or how often you take a shower after your run is irrelevant. That information doesn't help you assess your progress toward your 5K goal.

Well-designed, specific goals have clear, measurable signals, so you'll also want to celebrate small wins along the way, rather than holding out for a big reward at the end. Reward yourself after a full week of implementing a new habit, or when you reach ten percent of your goal. Find those partial wins, recognize them, and celebrate your progress.

Achievable

Ideally, the goals you set will push you out of your comfort zone in the pursuit of something positive. Maybe you'll explore a new pastime, such as painting or playing the piano, or add a positive habit, such as drinking sixty ounces of water daily or doing yoga regularly. As you're deciding on your goal(s), you'll want to make sure they are within reason, which means that they are possible.

Setting goals that are too ambitious will only result in disappointment. For example, deciding you want to be an astronaut at age seventy-five, or to try out for the San Francisco 49ers after a sedentary career in finance, may not be realistic. Are these goals impossible? Not necessarily, but realistically, they're not achievable in a year.

More common goals that may be achievable but not within a year's timeframe include mastering a foreign language by studying only on weekends, saving $1 million on a $50k salary, or traveling around the world on a $3,000 budget. Again, I can't say that they are absolutely impossible, but it's safe to say they would be challenging to achieve within 365 days.

To determine whether a goal is possible, you'll want to assess the resources available to support you and your commitment to the goal. Achievable goals are stretch goals—challenging but not out of reach. If you're not sure whether your goal is attainable, do some research to determine what it would take to reach it.

If you conclude that your goal is not achievable with your current resources, including time, money, skill, and attention, among other considerations, you need to modify your goal. Don't give up on it altogether; figure out what version of your goal is possible. Adapt it so that it is realistic and will still bring you joy, even if you don't accomplish the whole thing.

Maybe it's unrealistic to try to spend an entire summer in Italy if you only get two weeks of vacation at work and you need your job to live. Instead, explore what ten days or two weeks would look like and work toward that.

If you're having difficulty moving past the all-or-nothing mentality, where you won't be satisfied unless you get 100 percent of your goal, then you may not ever accomplish even a portion of it. You'll need to embrace a mindset adjustment and begin to think in terms of progress and not perfection. Few things in life are either/or, or black/white. Most of life is on the gray scale, and if you're unwilling to budge and adjust your planning, you won't make any change at all.

Relevant

Relevance is a little shorter and sweeter than the previous examples. It refers to the impact reaching your goal will have on your life and the extent to which it reflects your values. Simply ask yourself: *Will it make my life better? More fulfilling? Will it put me on a path to achieving my long-term goals?* Some goals, like saving money, may be small or medium, but they can help you reach larger goals, such as going back to school, adopting a baby, or buying a new home.

Time-bound

Perhaps most importantly, SMART goals have a due date or deadline. Having an ending point creates a sense of urgency and focus. There is a saying that "A goal is a wish with a deadline." Without a deadline, your goal is unlikely to be met.

With any goal, pick a date by which you want to have achieved it. Ideally, that deadline is realistic but bold. Meaning, it needs to be within the realm of possibility that you could complete it by the set date.

Pick a due date that pushes you to take advantage of your motivation now to secure some early wins. This deadline creates your map that leads to progress.

A Little More About the Element of Time

Time can either be your friend or your foe. Many people have a disconnect with the notion of time. They don't seem to understand how long it takes to do things. They seem unaware of their normal patterns and pace, which can lead them to set goals that ignore how quickly they typically work.

If it typically takes you an hour each morning to review and answer all your work emails, you should expect that to be the case in the future. Unfortunately, despite this data, some people will set goals assuming they can get through their emails in fifteen minutes each day. Since they are never able to get through their inbox in this amount of time, they're just setting themselves up for failure from the outset. Unless they've overhauled or delegated part of the process, there is no reason to expect that they can cut their email processing time by 75 percent overnight. It's not realistic.

If you recognize that you aren't 100 percent sure how long something is going to take, overestimate rather than underestimate. Give yourself more time than you think you'll need. It's much better to expect that it will take a year for you to achieve something and discover you can achieve it in ten months than to get a year out and see that you'll need more time. Be generous with how much time you give yourself because that extra time can help you mitigate any unexpected challenges that surface.

Underestimating the time to get something done can also make you feel like a failure, and that mindset really gets in the way of accomplishing goals. It's wiser to finish and see that you have time left over and that you did it in less time, than to go past your due date and then feel bad about it. That doesn't help anyone, and it could damage your self-esteem and determination.

Ultimately, many people who struggle with planning struggle with time management. That's actually one of the main reasons they don't plan—because they don't understand how to manage their time effectively.

Step 3: Identify Your Anchor—The Deep Reason Behind this Goal

Because commitment to a goal can wane over time, you must identify your anchor or your purpose. Your primary goal should be connected to your anchor, or your guiding principle. Why is this goal important to you? How will your life change when you accomplish it? Think back to the first chapter, where you envisioned your bigger life dreams. How does this goal help you get there? That's your anchor. Your anchor is what makes your goal meaningful to you beyond achieving it. It's a source of motivation when you start to doubt whether you can succeed. Refer back to it when your perseverance starts to fade. Remind yourself frequently of the impact attaining this goal will have on your quality of life.

Anchors Help You Stop the All-or-Nothing Mindset

Anchors keep you on track in the long term. At some point on your journey, you might feel frustrated and think your progress isn't happening quickly enough. You might tell yourself that if you are only making small steps forward, no one will notice, and it's not worth doing anymore. This is an all-or-nothing attitude that can be detrimental to goal setting and, more importantly, to goal attainment.

Without taking small steps, you'll be exactly where you are now in a year, and you don't want that. You won't necessarily be able to notice the progress you've made toward your goal in the first few weeks, but the more you remember your anchor and stick with your plan, the more successful you will be. This is not going to be a quick fix for your life, but it will undoubtedly get you to your goal.

Let's say your goal is to learn to speak Italian and that when you're sixty-five, you'll spend a summer in Italy to become fluent. But why wait until you're sixty-five? This is an all-or-nothing mentality: "If I can't travel to Italy until I retire, then there is no point in learning Italian until then."

Instead, how about starting to study Italian now, through an online program or even just studying basic vocabulary using flash cards? If you learned two new words a week, you would know 104 words by next year. In four years, you will know over four hundred words. Even while living your current life, you can still find ways to make progress toward what you dream about. And in that time, you can watch Italian movies, enjoy Italian restaurants, and meet other people who are trying to learn the language who you could practice with.

Having an anchor allows you to build momentum over time because every step you take toward your big goal is a step in the right direction. Start with the smallest increment you can commit to. Then commit to investing the time in doing that smallest increment. At first, you might feel like you're making no progress, but with a powerful anchor, you will eventually hit a tipping point where you can see how far you've come. You'll be able to look back at your starting point and recognize your growth and accomplishment. And I encourage you to stick with it even when it gets hard to keep going, because that's when the momentum kicks in and helps push you forward.

Final Thoughts About Your New Goal

When you set your goal, it's not enough to state what the goal is; you also need to describe how you'll feel when you accomplish it. How will your life be different? What will achieving the goal mean for other areas of your life? What will change?

Remember to practice visualization and imagine what it will look and feel like to achieve this particular goal. Rerun that same visualization as often as possible to help train your brain to find ways to help you achieve it.

Also, say your goal out loud. Repeat it to yourself, to remind yourself what you're aiming for. As the Buddha said, "What we think, we become," so make sure you are filling your mind with images, sounds, smells, and feelings associated with the attainment of that goal you've set.

Chapter Cheat Sheet

Step 1: Choose ONE primary goal that moves you closer to your envisioned life.

- If you have twenty things on your master list and you want them all, but you can only do one, ask yourself which one will make the most significant difference in improving your life next year?
- Which goal on your list will move you closer to that bigger, long-term vision you had for your life?

Step 2: Turn your goal into a SMART goal.

- Is my goal Specific, Measurable, Achievable, Relevant, and Time-bound?
- If my outcome is qualitative, how can I express it quantitatively so I can measure my success?

Step 3: Identify your anchor—the deep reason behind this goal.

Why is this goal important to you?

How will your life change when you accomplish it?

Mentor Notes & Insights

A Life Cleanse

When you get rid of a lot of the background noise in your life that is distracting you from your goal, it's much easier to focus on what you're trying to do and to make steady progress. Some of the items on your to-do list are interferences, and the quicker you take care of them, the faster you'll make progress. I like to call this clearing out of distractions a life cleanse.

When I say "life cleanse," I'm not talking about anything physical or medicinal. What I'm referring to is taking time to cross items off your to-do list that are stealing your attention. These include scheduling a dental appointment, filing an insurance claim or reimbursement request, or returning an online order. They can be very mundane, but until you do them, they will linger in your subconscious.

Or the tasks can be finance-related, such as setting up autopay for all your bills so you don't have to worry about making sure your payments are in on time, or organizing all your receipts and handing them to your accountant so they can start working on your taxes.

In this case, I'm not suggesting that you pay off all your bills and be done with them, partly because that's unrealistic and partly because that might interfere with your goal! What I'm really talking about here is simplifying all those pesky things you know you need to get done, but which pull your focus away from your goal. It's so easy to think that you can spend just a few minutes on one of those tasks, but suddenly two hours have passed and you've run out of time to even start work on your goal. That's what I don't want to happen, so use a life cleanse to organize all those background tasks and reduce the white noise that is in your way.

Personally, I'm a big fan of the life cleanse because it's a form of mental decluttering. Clean up your physical and subconscious environment so you can devote your time and attention to making progress.

When your mind and space are clear, there are far fewer hurdles to overcome on the path to your goal. And once those are gone, you can begin to introduce new habits and routines that support your goal.

CHAPTER 3

A—Analyze your Starting Point

Today, Chef Julia Child is synonymous with French cooking. But when she was in her thirties, she probably would never have guessed how radically her life would change from socialite to TV celebrity and published author. In 1948, at thirty-six, she moved from California to France when her husband was assigned to the U.S. Foreign Service in Paris.

One night, her foodie spouse took her out to dinner at a restaurant in Rouen, France called La Couronne, which she described as a religious experience because the food was so delicious.[1] The meal sparked a newfound fascination with cooking in her. Recognizing the only way to develop serious cooking skills was to take classes, she applied and was accepted to Le Cordon Bleu, a prestigious French cooking school.

Despite, or perhaps because of, being considerably older than other students and the only woman in her class, Child locked into her goal of becoming a successful chef. She was determined to succeed. However, she also accepted that she was starting from a disadvantage, due to her age, nationality, and lack of previous culinary training or experience. To compensate, she practiced various techniques for hours outside of class, took copious notes, and was determined to excel, continuing to learn and hone her skills post-graduation.

After culinary school, Child spent more than a decade cultivating her talent. She was determined to teach French cooking to American home cooks. She needed to analyze her starting point by assessing her strengths, weaknesses, opportunities, and threats. That assessment led her to realize she had passion, discipline, and top-notch training, but she was older than most TV cooks, lacked the typical TV personality, and had an unconventional background. So she started by co-authoring *Mastering the Art of French Cooking* with two other chefs.

Thanks to that publishing credit, she was invited to demonstrate how to make an omelet on Boston public television in 1962. The station got so much positive feedback from her appearance that they gave her a show of her own, *The French Chef,* the following year. Americans wanted cooking expertise that was easy to follow, and TV producers quickly saw her potential. That show made her famous.

Rather than trying to overhaul her image to become a traditional TV star, Child knew who she was and leaned into her awkwardness and eccentricities. She built on her warmth and casual manner to build a huge culinary brand.

Chapter Objective: By the end of this chapter, you will take an honest look at your current habits, routines, and mindset. You will identify your strengths and weaknesses, name at least one habit that holds you back, and choose the key changes you need to make to reach your goal.

Slow and Steady Wins the Race

Most people get inspired by a new goal and jump in with both feet to pursue it. Their excitement bubbles over as they begin their quest. Unfortunately, many ultimately fail to achieve their goal because they do not take their current situation into account. They are unrealistic about where they are starting from and become discouraged when they don't see immediate or long-lasting progress.

Julia Child recognized that, despite wanting to replicate the meal she had at La Couronne, she knew very little about cooking, much less French cooking. Recognizing this, she began exploring how to close the gap between boiling water and mastering a French delicacy. Her dedication and analysis of her current situation enabled her to attain the goal. She knew where she was starting from and where she wanted to go. This is what the PLAN to WIN can help you do, too.

This chapter will help you determine how to get from where you are now, Point A, to your goal, Point B.

But before you begin planning your future and what you want it to look like, you must stop and analyze where you are right now. Assess where you are starting from in relation to your bigger goal. Pausing to analyze your current situation before rushing ahead to design a roadmap to where you want to go will help ensure you take the quickest route and won't get lost or off track.

My Classroom Experience

Before making changes to my AP US History curriculum, I did a thorough SWOT analysis of my teaching. I found strengths in my experience, deep subject knowledge, and ability to engage students. My weaknesses stood out more: Both my students and I felt overwhelmed. Their skills developed unevenly, and I focused on covering the material rather than ensuring mastery.

Looking closely, I found opportunities in years of student performance data, common writing mistakes, and research on learning. The challenges were clear too: limited time, pressure to follow the curriculum, and the risk of burnout from trying to do too much. This analysis showed one key point: The problem wasn't a lack of effort or expertise, but a lack of a system to manage complexity.

Lisa's Journey

Before jumping into starting her catering business, Lisa honestly assessed her starting point. She had clear strengths: creativity, organization, a solid reputation, and years of executing successful events. However, she also faced weaknesses: limited time, inconsistent follow-through, and a tendency to prioritize urgent tasks over important ones. On the plus side, she enjoyed a supportive community, clear paths to licensing, and encouragement from trusted people. Yet she faced challenges that had held her back: burnout, decision fatigue, and fear of disruption. By taking the time to see things clearly, Lisa realized her issue wasn't a lack of effort or ability. It was the absence of a system to manage life's ups and downs.

Rebuild and Restore a Weakening Business

Sometimes you achieve a goal, move on, and are pulled back when things go haywire. That was the case for Howard Schultz, Starbucks' CEO. After establishing Starbucks as a ubiquitous brand in the 1980s and 1990s, he stepped down as CEO in 2000. However, he stepped back into the role in 2008, at age fifty-four, when the company began to struggle at the height of the Great Recession.

At the time, Starbucks had excellent brand recognition and loyal customers, and Schultz himself was well respected; however, the company's aggressive expansion in the early 2000s had weakened many aspects of its operations, including its culture. Schultz could see those strengths and weaknesses, as well as the opportunities and threats. To rebuild, which was his singular goal, he knew Starbucks would have to double down on service quality, customer experience, and corporate culture. By focusing on those elements, he was confident the company could address the threats it faced: declining customer trust, operational underperformance, and the recession already underway.

To kick off this turnaround, Schultz famously shuttered every Starbucks location in the US for one day to retrain and recalibrate the organization. He wanted to shock his team and underscore the importance of the basics. His approach worked, mainly because he first identified where the company and brand stood. He clarified the gap between where they were at that time and where they wanted to be and took action to close it.

To use a roadmap analogy, Schultz started by identifying which road Starbucks was on, then mapped out how it would reach its destination: increased profitability and growth. He didn't make assumptions about the problems; he researched and verified them. He was successful because he took stock of the current situation first.

The PLAN to WIN in Action

The same is true for your real-life plans—you need to know where you are and what limitations you're working with, like Schultz did, before you start. That way, you can find the path that gets you to your goal as quickly and efficiently as possible. So far, you've **Pictured** your ideal life and **Locked in** on one goal to pursue in the next year. Now it's time to **Analyze** your starting point before you strategize the best way to achieve the goal you've set.

Step 1: Honestly Assess Your Current Routines, Habits, and Patterns Using the AWARE Scan

This step focuses on self-awareness, a core component of mindfulness practice. A mindfulness practice is about being present and not judging yourself. Self-awareness comes from this. It's about understanding your personal patterns.

Many people think they know where they are in relation to their life goals, but they don't take the time to examine their habits, beliefs, and mindset. That's where their strengths and weaknesses lie, which will shape how their plan goes.

When you pause to assess where you are in your efforts to reach your goals, you also need to think about the overall environment you've created, the emotions that you have about certain things, and the roadblocks you've previously faced that have gotten in the way of you achieving your goals. This is important if you want to move past those obstacles.

Let's say you decide on your birthday that you're going to read fifty-two books in the coming year. Before getting started, it would be worthwhile to consider how many books you read on average each year, to see what the gap is between where you are starting and the goal you have set. Are you a fast reader or a slow one? If you have set this goal before and been unsuccessful, why do you think that happened? For example, did you suddenly get busy and miss a couple of books? Did you start reading something you didn't like, so you stopped altogether?

You need to pause and analyze who you are, where you are skill-wise, your habits, your boundaries, and your mindset to set yourself up for success. You may be super-motivated and energetic today, but what happens when that energy wears off? It's not sustainable unless you have a plan to carry you through low-energy days.

Picturing Your Success is the fun part. Visualizing your ideal future and achieving your goal is typically easy. Everyone loves to do that; it's like daydreaming that you win the lottery. But success requires more than just visualization—once you have a clear picture, you need to take action. In chapter 2, you locked in a goal and chose one to start with. As you move forward in pursuing it, analyzing where you start from in relation to your goal is a mindfulness practice that few people pause to consider.

Missing this piece is what trips everyone up when life happens. That's why **A**, analyzing your starting point, is so critical. What people usually do is picture their success, lock into their goal, and then jump right into implementing the plan. They skip several steps entirely, leaping from vision to action. That's why their momentum fizzles.

That's what happens every year at New Year's. The Baylor College of Medicine found that **88** percent of people who set New Year's resolutions fail within the first two weeks.[2] The Ohio State University backs this up, reporting that only around 9 percent of people make it to the end of the year with their resolutions; 91 percent fail.[3]

But setting year-long goals is ideal for building the life you want. Keep in mind that this is a continuous improvement process, with new goals being modified or added to the old ones.

If your goal is to run a mile, for instance, once you can do that, you might set a new goal, such as a 5K (3.1 miles). Then, when you reach that goal, you might see that you love running and decide your goal is to run a mile every day for a month, or maybe this running goal was part of a bigger goal to get healthy, and you decide to keep running while starting to work on your nutrition.

The value of this PLAN to WIN system is that you keep improving on the last goal; you're constantly bettering yourself and your life through goal setting, planning, and building on your past successes.

You've probably noticed that I'm recommending more analytical tools at this point, and that's primarily because, in order to move ahead, you need to do more self-reflection. You'll set more realistic goals and can get a better handle on what needs to happen by using the AWARE scan and SWOT analyses, which are all about understanding yourself better. We're now shifting from the external perspective on what you want to achieve to evaluating what's possible given your internal skills and mindset.

Become More AWARE

One tool I created to help you get clear about where you are with respect to the one-year goal you've chosen is the AWARE Self-Scan framework, which breaks down your current habits and situation. This scan is an original framework, informed by the work of Susan David and Jon Kabat-Zinn, as well as contemporary behavior change research.

The purpose of the questions in the AWARE Scan is to help you conduct a deep self-assessment. What are your daily routines and habits? Do they support the goal you've set for yourself or not? If not, what changes can you make to improve your odds of achieving your goal? If you can identify the mindset, habits, and behaviors that are standing in your way, your odds of attaining your goal go way, way up. So, complete the scan, then ask yourself: *What do I notice about how I* actually *spend my time, energy, money, and attention right now? What does my AWARE scan show about my* real *life, not an ideal version?*

AWARE Self-Scan

A: ARRIVE IN THE MOMENT

1. What is actually true about my weekly routines (wake, work, move, eat, sleep)?

2. Where did my time/energy/attention/money go in the last 7 days?

3. What one behavior most contradicts my stated goal?

4. When do I feel most resourceful during a typical day?

W: WITNESS YOUR MINDSET WITHOUT JUDGEMENT

5. What thoughts arise when I picture doing the next tiny step?

6. What emotions show up right before I self-sabotage?

7. What stories do I tell myself about "why it won't work"?

8. What would a neutral observer say I did yesterday to advance my goal?

A: ALLOW WHAT IS

9. Which constraints are non-negotiable (kids, shift work, health, budget)?

10. Which constraints are self-imposed (perfectionism, all-or-nothing rules)?

11. What craving/urge typically precedes the off-plan choice?

12. If today is a "bad" day, what's the smallest non-zero action I can still allow?

AWARE Self-Scan

R: ROOT YOURSELF IN YOUR REALITY

13. What three strengths friends would say I have (ask them)?

14. What cue → routine → reward loop drives the habits I want to change?

15. What replacement routine could give the same reward?

16. What environment tweak removes friction (layout, apps, people, time of day)?

E: ENGAGE MINDFULLY

17. What will I do when resistance appears?

18. What's my "pause, don't regress" plan on overwhelm days?

19. Who will I message after I finish (accountability)?

20. What will I review weekly to adjust the course?

Step 2: Identify One Habit or Pattern that Goes Against Your Goal

You may see yourself a certain way, but if you look more closely at how you behave and recognize that you sleep in late, avoid exercise, and eat junk food, you'll have to admit that is who you are right now. That's not who you have to be forever, but your current lifestyle will determine, to some degree, how easy it will be to reach your goal.

If one of your goals is to get healthy and eat more vegetables, once you analyze where you are with respect to that goal, you can begin to identify the habit changes you need to make to get there. Or, if your goal is to start a business or write a book, maybe what's holding you back isn't existing bad habits, but a lack of clarity about how to even start.

Using a weight-loss example, if you keep saying you want to lose sixty pounds, but you sleep in late, sit at a desk all day, and then come home and eat junk food, it should be pretty obvious why you may be having difficulty losing weight. Your habits don't match your goal.

To change, you first need to accept that's who you are right now—a sedentary night owl who appreciates tasty junk food (and really, who doesn't?!). Only then can you start changing your identity and habits. You can ask, "Why do I come home every day and eat junk?" Then explore what the cues are. Could it be that your days are so stressful that by the time you get home, you need a dopamine hit? Or is it simply that you're so hungry at that point that you aren't willing to spend time making a healthy meal? It's important to really think about *why* you do what you do so you can address it.

Habits expert Charles Duhigg will tell you you're much more likely to successfully change a habit when you identify the cue and reward and then change the behavior. Holding the cue and the reward the same, you find a different way to address it. So, if you're stressed at the end of the day and you need a dopamine hit, instead of eating junk food, you can listen to some of your favorite music, meditate, pet your dog, or go for a brisk fifteen-minute walk. That way, you change the habit and get the same reward, a dopamine hit, just in a different, healthier form.

Habit Loop Swap Example: Cue (e.g., end-of-day stress) → new routine (15-min walk, pet the dog, listen to music, meditate 5-min) → same reward (dopamine).

Some people will claim that trading a bag of salty snacks for a long walk at the end of a stressful day at work isn't realistic. The snacks are so tempting and right in front of them, while the walk is much less tempting. They may convince themselves it's too dark, too late, too cold, or too lonely to go for a walk, for example. These are real obstacles, which is why it is crucial to find a replacement habit that feels just as easy and rewarding as the original.

Another option is to continue exploring other potential behaviors and eventually find the right habit loop swap that helps you change and move closer to your goal. There are plenty of alternative ways to get that dopamine hit besides a walk. But you first have to analyze what your actions are right now, what your behavior has been, and where you are trying to get to. And unfortunately, many people aren't honest with themselves about this. They have an ideal version of themselves in their head, or maybe a version of who they used to be, but that's not actually how they behave now. So ask yourself: *What do I recognize about the habits that hold me back? What is one pattern I could change to make progress toward my big goal?*

Step 3: Complete a Lifestyle SWOT

Now that you have a good handle on your mindset, habits, behaviors, and identified a habit loop swap, it's time to consider what you do well (your strengths), and where you could use some support (your weaknesses). We all have a laundry list of strengths and weaknesses, some of which we know about ourselves and others we may be reluctant to admit.

A tool for clarifying your personal strengths and weaknesses is a Lifestyle SWOT analysis, originally developed by Albert S. Humphrey at Stanford Research Institute. SWOT stands for Strengths, Weaknesses, Opportunities, and Threats. It's primarily used in business, but it can also apply here as you start to identify the best path to achieving your goal.

Lifestyle SWOT

STRENGTHS
EXISTING HABITS / SKILLS (E.G., EARLY RISER)

WEAKNESSES
REPEAT PATTERNS (E.G., SCROLLING ON PHONE FOR HOURS)

OPPORTUNITIES
LEVERAGE POINTS (E.G., SUPPORTIVE COLLEAGUE)

THREATS
PREDICTABLE ROADBLOCKS (TRAVEL, SICK, KIDS)

WILL CHANGE NOW	WILL DESIGN AROUND

Make a list of each of these SWOT categories, starting with your Strengths: what you're good at or what habits and skills are beneficial to you. Then explore your Weaknesses: habits that are barriers to success. These are internal characteristics. Opportunities are your support system or resources that will help you make progress; they are external. The same applies to Threats, which are external roadblocks that could hinder your success.

Sometimes it's hard to know what you don't know. That's why asking yourself questions can be a good approach to discovering facts about yourself that you hadn't previously considered or recognized. Questions can give you a new perspective on who you are. So, ask yourself: *What are my strengths, weaknesses, opportunities, and threats right now? How can I use this understanding to make a PLAN to WIN that helps me achieve my goal this year?*

As you assess your responses to the questions I've shared in the AWARE Scan, it's very important that you review the answers without judgment. Don't agonize over your weaknesses. In fact, you shouldn't think of them as negatives at all. These are simply data points about yourself—little pieces of information that help you recognize what you do that is allowing you to progress toward your goal and what you are doing that may be getting in the way. Try not to think of them as good or bad, only as clues.

This assessment is designed to prepare you to start listing the steps you'll need to take to reach your goal. But before you can begin, you need to be crystal clear about which tasks will be easy for you and which activities may be more challenging or require a new approach altogether.

This is the point at which you figure out what you're dealing with on your road to your goal. To use a roadmap analogy, let's say you're doing your pre-trip check. You're making sure your tires have the correct pressure, that the oil has been changed, that you have a full tank of gas or a full electrical charge, that you have windshield wiper fluid, snacks, and anything else you may want to examine. If you don't check how ready your vehicle is for the trip, you're likely to encounter a setback along the way.

Step 4: Ask Three to Five Trusted People for Feedback About Your Strengths and Blind Spots

During this time of self-reflection and identifying the habits that may have previously gotten in the way of your reaching your goals, it can also be helpful to get an outside perspective. After you've completed your own self-reflection, consider asking three to five of your closest friends and family to tell you what they think your three strengths and three weaknesses are.

Be clear with them up front that you're not looking for them to be harsh or brutally honest, but to share how they see you—both your best qualities and maybe those they don't love as much. You want them to be honest with you while also protecting your feelings. You don't want to feel attacked. So be sure to determine who you trust enough to ask what your best and not-so-great qualities are.

The things they'll point out will likely be characteristics or flaws that you are already aware of, but it can be helpful for others to hold up a mirror to your personality. They may see something in you that you were totally blind to, which can spark new ideas for careers or hobbies or for overcoming resistance in reaching your goal.

I did this exercise last year with a few of my closest friends and my sister, and the number one thing everyone said was that I was good at planning and organization. That's where the idea for this book originated, which pushed me to start brainstorming how I could package what I love to do so I could share it with more people. That's the value of asking others to tell you what they think you're good at and where you might be running into trouble with respect to goal attainment. Ask yourself: *How can I stay open to their feedback to help me see patterns I couldn't see on my own?*

Step 5: Choose One or Two Key Adjustments to Support your Goal

Keep in mind that as you assess how you're currently living your life and consider any changes you may want to make, you don't need an immediate overhaul. Don't try to change too much all at once; slow and steady wins the race.

If your goal is to get healthier and your first milestone is to stop drinking soda, but you currently drink five sodas a day, your first change should probably be to cut back from five to four, maybe replacing the extra one with water. Then, over time, reduce it from four to three, so that you're making steady, small wins that don't impact your life all that much. Those small, incremental changes are easier to make and easier to stick with. Trying to quit soda cold turkey in one fell swoop is much more difficult, and you're less likely to be successful because it's such a radical change from what you're used to. It's always better to adjust your behavior gradually than to do a 180 and have to admit failure soon thereafter. Ask yourself: *What is one small change I can implement to make reaching my goal a little easier?*

After you've weaned yourself off soda, maybe you decide to add a cup of vegetables to one meal a day. After just a month, you've now had thirty more cups of vegetables than you did in previous months. You're already behaving so much healthier and are on your way to achieving your goal with these minor adjustments, small changes, and course corrections.

With a year-long goal, one month of progress means you're at least one twelfth of the way there. You've made good progress, but you're not expected to hit your goal in only thirty days, or even ninety days. You're working toward a 365-day goal. At each step of the way, you're going to keep improving on the progress you've made, potentially even going beyond that original goal.

Take starting a business as another example. If your goal is to start a new business and leave your current job in a year, then once you succeed, you don't just close your business, you set a new goal to strive for. Maybe your goal is to hit a specific revenue target in your first year, or win an industry award, or hire your first employee. But you won't be able to do that if you sit back and revel in the fact that you're now a new business owner. You need to keep putting in time and effort to continue to build your business so it succeeds.

Chapter Cheat Sheet

Step 1: Honestly assess your current routines, habits, and patterns using the AWARE scan.

- What are your daily habits and routines?
- What does your AWARE scan show about your real life, not an ideal version?

Step 2: Identify one habit or pattern that goes against your goal.

- What do you recognize about the habits that hold you back?
- What is one pattern you could change to make progress toward your big goal?

Step 3: Complete a Lifestyle SWOT (Strengths, Weaknesses, Opportunities, Threats).

- What are your strengths, weaknesses, opportunities, and threats right now?
- How can I use this understanding to make a PLAN to WIN that helps me achieve my goal this year?

Step 4: Ask three to five trusted people for feedback about your strengths and blind spots.

- Who do you trust enough to ask what your best and not-so-great qualities are?
- How will you stay open to their feedback to help you see patterns you couldn't see on your own?

Step 5: Choose one or two key adjustments to your identity or routines that will support this goal.

- Ask yourself: *What is one small change I can implement to make reaching my goal a little easier?*
- What would your life look like if you adopted even one new identity statement ("I am the kind of person who . . .") that aligns with your goal?

Mentor Notes & Insights

Wanting More, Delayed Gratification, and the Power of Mindfulness

The need for increasing levels of satisfaction is part of being human. No matter what you give a human being, as soon as they have it, they will no longer be satisfied with it. It's a lot like lifestyle inflation, where you thought that huge raise you received last year would change your life, but then you upgraded your car, took a vacation, bought some new furniture, and suddenly you feel just as financially strapped as you did pre-promotion. Once you've experienced that additional money, you no longer appreciate it. It becomes the new level to which you're accustomed, and you want more.

The official term for this is the "hedonic treadmill,"[4] which says that after a positive or negative life event, that new level of satisfaction becomes our new baseline. Over time, we adjust our expectations so that our new, higher level of satisfaction or fulfillment is our new normal, and then we want more.

It's also hard to delay gratification. We humans not only want more, we want it now. The famous marshmallow experiment demonstrated this in 1970, when Professor Walter Mischel and his graduate students set up an experiment involving preschoolers.[5] The children were offered one marshmallow right away or two marshmallows if they were willing to wait for an adult who had left the room to return (this was about fifteen minutes, but the children didn't know this). Some kids wanted that single marshmallow immediately, while others were willing to hold out for a bigger payoff.

The researchers followed the children for decades after this initial marshmallow experiment. The results showed that children who were willing to wait for two marshmallows, demonstrating the ability to delay gratification and self-control at a young age, had more positive outcomes later in life, including "higher test scores, healthier lifestyles, lower BMI, and stronger social skills." Although these conclusions can be partially attributed to socioeconomic status, they do illustrate that self-control provided advantages throughout childhood and young adulthood, leading to greater career and relationship success.

The ability to delay gratification is a skill that can be learned. So, if you can learn to delay immediate gratification for the gratification you will receive when you reach your ultimate goal, you are more likely to have compounded success. This can be seen as another mindfulness challenge: You have to push past negative emotions and frustrations that arise and keep sticking with your plan. Sometimes that includes admitting that you're uncomfortable and recognizing that this discomfort stems from the changes we must make to achieve our goals. Change is difficult, even when we want the outcome it will bring us. Those who can't break out of the cycle of needing immediate gratification, who can't wait to get the two marshmallows, are more likely to abandon their goal.

Mindfulness is a key practice to break out of those old habits. One of my favorite insights from mindfulness is that your emotions are like weather patterns, constantly changing. It's never rained forever, it's never been cloudy forever, and it's never been sunny forever, so whatever weather pattern you're experiencing now, it will pass. No matter what you're feeling in the moment, you will eventually have a new emotion. If you're feeling angry, it may take an hour to get past it, or maybe a week, but eventually you will feel different. You have to ride it out to get the two marshmallows. If you can't let discomfort happen in your life, then you probably won't achieve big goals.

It's important to become comfortable with discomfort. You've probably heard the saying that "Obesity is hard. Being healthy is hard." Or, "Starting a business is hard. Working a 9-to-5 is hard." Choose your hard.

In this case, it may take a month, or even several, of discomfort because you're doing something really big to change your life. But if you can weather this storm and remember your anchor, the goal will be achieved, and it will all have been worth it.

If you've decided to stop extra spending to be able to pay off a debt, that season of austerity may not be fun, but the outcome will be. Or if you're saving to make a home down payment in a year, you may not be happy to give up your annual summer vacation or your season sports tickets, but that temporary period of changing your spending habits will reap big rewards.

The good news is that after you've changed your habits consistently for a few weeks, the rewards start trickling in. Especially after ninety days, you'll begin to see progress, whether it's the size of your savings account balance rising or the scale you're standing on. You'll see incremental evidence of the positive changes you've made long before you reach your goal.

In weight loss, there is a saying that you will notice positive changes in four weeks, that people close to you will notice in eight weeks, and that acquaintances will notice in twelve weeks, which is right around the ninety-day mark I mentioned. Those changes that you start to see will be enough of a reward to get you through that next month, or next quarter, when you'll continue to see evidence of even more progress. That success compounds, and your discomfort becomes a little easier once you get into that flow state. You'll have momentum pushing you forward with less and less discomfort.

CHAPTER 4

N—NAME THE ELEMENTS

Bernard "Bernie" Marcus planned Home Depot's launch for years before taking the leap. Marcus had risen through the ranks at several retail-related companies, including Vornado, O'Dell, and Handy Dan, where he became CEO. During his tenure at Handy Dan, a California home-improvement chain, he started with four locations and expanded the operation to eighty stores.[1]

Along the way, Marcus conceived of a new kind of home improvement store that would compete on volume through hefty discounts and a broad selection of products. He and colleague Arthur Blank, who worked with him at Handy Dan, **Pictured** their success and **Locked in** on a goal of starting a new retail chain. Their vision was a discount retailer with a larger footprint than any competitor, a massive inventory of products, well-trained customer service staff, and the financial capital to dominate the markets it entered.[2] They

Analyzed their starting point and began planning how they could bring this vision to life.

Next, they needed to **Name** the elements: what they would need to know and be able to do to proceed with creating this new business, including vendors, a large retail space, knowledgeable employees, and the financial backing to place large inventory orders.

Then, without notice, both men were let go from Handy Dan as part of a turnaround plan.[3] That situation actually made it easier for Marcus and Blank to begin work in earnest on their plan for a chain of home-improvement supercenters. Because they had already identified all the elements needed to bring their vision to reality, they were able to write out the steps in a logical sequence and implement their plan successfully. The first Home Depot store opened in Atlanta in 1979, went public in 1981, and, as of 2025, was the world's largest home improvement retailer.

None of this happened because Marcus and Blank were just bold risk-takers. It happened because they worked hard to figure out what it would take to succeed before building. They identified the knowledge, resources, skills, and conditions needed to move forward. This turned their bold vision into a plan they could follow. Now, you can do the same, by building your goal on preparation instead of hope.

Chapter Objective: By the end of this chapter, you will clearly name the elements that you must know, have, or be able to do to reach your goal. You will write down everything you need to know or do before taking action.

How Naming Can Help

First, I want to acknowledge that this is the shortest chapter, and that's intentional. The "*Name* the Elements" step focuses on clarifying the required components to achieve the goal rather than making decisions or plans. This is sometimes called preparatory planning or cognitive offloading.

Research on **preparatory planning** by health psychologist **Ralf Schwarzer** of Freie Universität Berlin shows that identifying what you need before planning leads to better follow-through than jumping right into action.

Additionally, studies by **Roy Baumeister** of Florida State University and **Michael Scullin** of Baylor University on **cognitive and intention offloading** reveal that writing down your needs and unfinished tasks lowers mental load and helps you focus better on execution. In short, naming required skills, resources, constraints, and supports shifts how your brain views the goal.

Though this step is brief, it is crucial. By making hidden requirements visible, "*Name* the Elements" sets the stage for the rest of the PLAN to WIN system to operate with more clarity, less friction, and greater realism.

My Classroom Experience

As I revamped the AP US History course, I didn't jump right in to rewriting lessons or creating a new syllabus. I stepped back to identify what was needed for a successful redesign. This wasn't just planning; it was about recognizing requirements. I listed the course's instructional needs, including identifying clear outcomes, ideas for purposeful lessons to practice these expectations, and assessments to see if the expectations were met along the way.

I also thought about how difficult the school year can seem at times, with the various events and illnesses that disrupt the flow of progress, and how, during these times, decision fatigue can affect consistency. Having a solid, thoughtful structure in place matters more than motivation for sustaining effort. Only after naming these elements could I properly organize and sequence the course. I wasn't just redesigning it; I was setting the stage for consistent progress. By naming the elements first, I would be able to build a system that worked to meet the goal, not just one that looked good on paper.

Lisa's Journey

With a clear starting point, Lisa paused before writing out the steps of her plan to make a list of what she needed to know or be able to do to launch her catering business. This list wasn't a plan; it was an inventory of considerations.

She started with practical details, such as an understanding of local regulations, how to price her services competitively, how to create a simple list of menu packages, and how to carve out time for planning during her busy weeks. At this stage, nothing was organized yet. Still, by naming these elements, both obvious and previously unknown, Lisa gained clarity. This helped her prepare to organize and prioritize her tasks effectively.

Naming For Success

Perhaps best known for the blockbuster Fantastic Four comic series, Stan Lee, born Stanley Lieber, rose in the ranks of comics publishing. Early in his career, there was constant demand for comic book content, such as Captain America and other superheroes, but over time, Lee grew tired of churning out the same old stories.

"We're writing nonsense. It's a stupid business for a grown-up to be in," he complained to his wife,[4] as he began to conceive of comics with a message, featuring flawed characters. He wanted the creative autonomy to break free of churning out predictable stories featuring superhuman characters that few could relate to.

He **Pictured** his characters as more human than invincible, and, on the brink of quitting his job, he **Locked in** on a goal: producing a different kind of story. Following his wife's advice, he determined that he wanted to make comics that not only entertained but also educated. He **Analyzed** his current situation and decided he needed to take a risk before just quitting his job.

Rather than jumping into the creative process or getting lost down a rabbit hole of organizing the bookkeeping for his new venture, he paused to **Name** the elements first—identifying everything he would need to know and be able to do for this new idea to come to life. These elements included exploring the new types of stories he wanted to tell, as well as the logistics of going in this new direction. Ultimately, he wrote his own unique comic, which became the Fantastic Four. It was a major hit and transformed the entire comic book industry. Other characters he created through the years include Spider-Man, Iron Man, the Hulk, Thor, and many more. As the *Los Angeles Review of Books* explained, "Lee's stories would incorporate relatable characters and current events, combining the fantastic and the everyday."[5]

Stan Lee's success didn't come from working harder or being more creative. It came from taking a moment to name the elements of success. You can do the same. Before you act, list everything you need to know, decide, or be able to do to reach your goal. Include skills, resources, capabilities, and constraints. For now, though, avoid organizing or creating timelines. By identifying these elements, you can turn a vague idea into a clear plan. This simple step can turn a theoretical idea into reality.

<u>The PLAN to WIN in Action</u>

Now it's your turn to **Name** the elements: everything you must know, have, or be able to do for the goal to be possible.

Step 1(The Only Step): Brain-Dump All of the Tasks, Skills, and Experiences You Think Are Required to Reach Your Goal

Think of all of the little things you will need to know and be able to do in order to reach the bigger goal you locked in on. Often, when we try new things, we don't know what we don't know. If this is how you're feeling, to get started, you might ask the following:

- What are the first five things someone would Google if they wanted to do this?
- Who are three people who have already done this that I could

research to learn how?

- What are the major categories of work involved to make this happen (e.g., legal, financial, creative, etc.)?

Take a few minutes to brainstorm and fill up the page with everything that comes to mind.

Chapter Cheat Sheet

Brain-dump all the tasks, skills, and experiences you think are required to reach your goal.

- What do I need to know to accomplish my goal?
- Can I be okay with my list of requirements feeling exhaustive, even if messy at this point?

Mentor Notes & Insights

Find Your People

As you pursue your goal, you may also need to adjust your inner circle. It is often said that you are the average of the five people you spend the most time with, a claim attributed to a wide variety of people, from the Buddha to motivational speaker Jim Rohn. So, ask yourself: *Are the five people closest to me my role models? Do I want to become more like them? Do I admire them?* And if your honest answer to those questions is "no," then you may need to reevaluate your friend group and make some new connections.

Because very rarely do you see a group of five friends who are not alike in some core way. You're much more likely to find a group who are all athletic, or all obese, or all super successful, or all from the same neighborhood. They have things in common. What you probably won't see is a group of five friends where one is training for a triathlon, one is obese, one is a grandmother, one is the CEO of a multinational corporation, and the fifth is unhoused. Most friend groups consist of people with the same socioeconomic status, the same general education level, and the same season of life. There may be a little diversity, but not to a great extent.

So, if you're feeling unsupported, unmotivated, or not in sync with your current friend group, branch out. Look for people who are more like you. Maybe they have the same hobbies, interests, or current goals. For example, if you want to start a business but no one in your life is an entrepreneur, find a group where you can connect with other entrepreneurs. Or maybe you enjoy knitting, but none of your friends knit. So, find a group of knitters where you can be around like-minded people.

You need to surround yourself with people who understand your goal, support you, and create an environment where you are uplifted and inspired to work toward it. If you do that, achieving your goal will become much easier.

What gets written gets clearer.
—Anne Lamott

CHAPTER 5

W—WRITE IT OUT

Known as the architect of the West Coast Offense in football, famed San Francisco 49ers coach Bill Walsh led his team to three Super Bowl victories in the 1980s. Early in his career, working alongside coaches from other National Football League (NFL) teams, Walsh witnessed the value of scripting plays in advance and planning out exactly how the game could unfold well before the coin toss. This was an innovative approach at the time.

Walsh once explained the impact of the West Coast Offense, as it became known: "What we have finally done is rehearse the opening part of the game, almost the entire first half, by planning the game before it even starts."[1] Walsh believed in the power of writing out the steps before implementing the plan, and that practice turned his goal into wins over and over again.

What started as scripting three plays for the quarterback to call while he was with the Cincinnati Bengals grew to ten plays with the

San Diego Chargers, twenty plays while coaching at Stanford, and then twenty-five scripted plays with the San Francisco 49ers. By **Writing** out every step to take, in order, and creating milestones for the concepts, drills, and game plans needed to accomplish the goal, a nearly unstoppable football dynasty was created.

Walsh's **Picture** of success was a winning football team. He **Locked in** on the goal of creating a championship system. He **Analyzed** the gaps to be filled based on the team's on-field skills. He **Named** the elements required to be successful, and then scaffolded milestones, such as teaching drills and concepts to help team members build strength and master the plays, to develop leaders, and to document each aspect of the plan. And he **Wrote** out the exact steps for every play so the team could prepare for the next game. When the 49ers entered the stadium before a game, they typically knew what was about to happen and how the game would progress because of Walsh's methodical planning.

Chapter Objective: By the end of this chapter, you will create a realistic schedule for the year, including quarterly and monthly overviews, as well as a detailed plan for your first week.

Writing it All Down—Turning the Elements into Action

Let's review everything you've already decided. You've already decided what success looks like to you, what goal you're going to focus on, and what your starting point strengths and weaknesses are. You've also named everything you need to know or be able to do to accomplish the goal. Now, you're going to write out the framework for your year, plotting milestones into each quarter and/or month, and plan out your day-to-day tasks for your first week.

What we are talking about in this step is specifically writing out your plan on paper. By committing your plan to paper, research shows that you are more likely to stick with your goal and achieve it. Sure, electronic planners are great, but it turns out that the physical act of handwriting makes a big difference. In a recent study at Baylor University[2], researchers Yanliu Huang, Zhen Yang, and Vicki G. Morwitz evaluated the value of using a physical calendar. They noted that although only 28 percent of people use a paper planner and 72 percent use an electronic planner on a phone or computer, "A higher percentage of paper calendar users completed the activity as compared to mobile users."

A study by Gail Matthews at Dominican University[3] also supports the idea that writing out the steps and committing to a goal makes a difference. Matthews' study found that 76 percent of participants who wrote down their goals and committed to taking action toward them achieved them. In contrast, only 43 percent of participants with goals who did not write them down were successful.

For this step in the PLAN to WIN system, you're going to take the elements that you named in the last chapter and put them into categories. Then you will identify milestones, put them in a logical order, and use backward design to lay out your plan and schedule it in your planner or calendar. For your schedule, you could maintain a regular cadence, such as weekly or monthly, or use a task-based approach. What you choose will depend on what makes sense for the goal you've set. This is a big step, and the most important for action to begin.

The milestones you choose will serve as smaller targets you achieve along the way to the final reward of accomplishing your big goal. By setting smaller targets, your brain releases dopamine every time you complete a task. This reward chemical reinforces motivation. Research from the University of Chicago confirmed that smaller steps that move you closer to your goal provide a visible sense of progress and that motivation rises as you approach each milestone.[4]

If your goal is to lose one hundred pounds in the next year, don't wait to celebrate until you've lost all one hundred pounds, because that's too far in the future. Instead, notice and celebrate all of the interim wins, such as losing your first ten pounds or fitting into an outfit you haven't worn for years. Or you could celebrate non-scale victories, such as running a mile or dropping down a clothing size.

If your goal is to go back to school to earn a degree, waiting until graduation to celebrate is too far off to be a meaningful reward or motivator. In the meantime, you could celebrate the completion of each course or semester.

Physical Planners vs. Digital Planners

If you're still trying to get your scheduling done with a digital planner, consider using it only for reminders and get a paper planner to map out the steps you need to take to reach your goal. I'm a big proponent of digital planners for everyday time management, but I would argue that writing everything out first in a physical planner is best. Then, if it helps you stay on top of your schedule, you can transfer your daily tasks and appointments into your digital calendar.

Research shows that handwriting activates more complex brain networks than typing, particularly in areas tied to learning, memory, and attention. The slower, more deliberate pace forces deeper processing, turning ideas into understanding rather than just entries on a screen.

A recent study from the Norwegian University of Science and Technology (NTNU) demonstrates that handwriting creates richer neural connectivity than keyboard use, supporting better retention and cognitive engagement.[5]

Physical planners excel at removing digital distractions—no notifications, no tab-switching—making planning a mindful, focused activity rather than a fragmented one. They also support deep thinking, long-term goal achievement, and memory formation. Additionally, writing goals and tasks by hand also increases psychological ownership and makes it feel more real, which strengthens follow-through.

Digital planners excel at speed, automation, and shared scheduling, but often encourage shallow engagement. The bottom line is that digital tools are efficient for logistics, but physical planners are superior for thinking, learning, and achieving meaningful goals.

How Writing Helps Avoid Decision Fatigue

When you write out and order the steps, you save yourself cognitive effort on a day-to-day basis because you've done much of the decision-making up front. People are cognitive misers by natural design—we are always looking for the easy way to do or decide anything. It's how we are wired.

So, when we think about big plans and goals, especially those that are long-term and transformational, and wonder why they aren't achieved, it's partly because we experience decision fatigue. We get tired of having to make decision after decision every day, which leads to quitting or giving up. By planning how to reach a goal from start to finish and putting effort into decision-making at the outset, when you are most excited about your transformation and most motivated, you eliminate decision fatigue later in the process. You've already mapped out your route, and all you need to do is start driving according to the plan you've designed.

It's incredibly easy to get overwhelmed by decision fatigue, where the quality of the decisions you're making declines over time. This can happen when there are too many decisions to make or when you are too tired from everyday tasks to make them. The PLAN to WIN addresses this issue in a game-changing way, so you don't have to rely on motivation to make decisions every day; you just need to follow the steps you've written out.

How To Make Progress Manageable

Big goals are usually made up of smaller, connected steps. When you can see these steps clearly, you can track your progress and feel like your efforts are paying off. For example, someone training for a marathon doesn't start by running 26.2 miles. They begin by building habits like walking regularly, eating better, and gradually building up to running, then running longer distances. Each step prepares them for the next one.

This idea is similar to psychologist Lev Vygotsky's Zone of Proximal Development (ZPD), which holds that growth occurs when a challenge is difficult but not too difficult. Usually, this zone is supported by temporary help or guidance. The PLAN to WIN system uses a similar idea but in a different way. Instead of relying on constant help, it uses smaller goals to help people find their way. These smaller goals don't do the work for you, but they show you that your work is working.

By focusing on the next important step rather than the whole journey, smaller goals help reduce feelings of overwhelm, build confidence by showing progress, and help you keep going over time. That's why this matters. When you can see your progress and have a plan, even big goals seem possible.

My Classroom Experience

When writing the steps for my new course, I had to keep in mind that in AP US History, the first two units cover only about 10 percent of the AP exam. So, I use these first few weeks as a training ground. At this stage, students are learning about classroom expectations and how to study effectively at the AP level. I focus on how building key habits, such as note-taking, sourcing documents, managing deadlines, and embracing productive struggle, can lead to long-term success. By the time we dive into tougher material, students have the skills they need. They aren't just handling more information; they have the tools to manage it. Writing out the course in this order prepares students for complexity before things get tough. It sets us both up for a smoother pace as the year progresses.

Lisa's Journey

When Lisa, the aspiring caterer, started writing out her steps, she first prioritized the tasks. She figured out what needed to be done now and what could wait. She began with simple steps, such as researching licensing requirements and defining her services. Once those were complete, she moved on to more challenging tasks, such as marketing, booking clients, and finding food service vendors. Writing out the steps in this order allowed her to achieve early success, build confidence and momentum, and avoid stress. With her steps in place, Lisa avoided having to wonder what to work on next. The plan already addressed this, allowing her to make progress even during low-energy weeks.

Tolkien's Unconventional Approach to Telling a Story

Writer J.R.R. Tolkien spent an estimated seventeen years conceptualizing and developing *The Lord of the Rings* trilogy, beginning in 1937. To tell the story he had **Pictured**, he **Locked in** the goal of finishing his book without compromising his vision of success, regardless of how long it took. He **Analyzed** what he would need to complete the story and then **Named** all of the elements necessary for his picture to come to life. Then he **Wrote** all the steps out in phases so that no detail would be lost. Through the years, he tweaked and recalibrated elements of the book, working in modules as milestones. He tied together story segments, adding increasing levels of detail and complexity.

As Tolkien once wrote to novelist Naomi Mitchison in 1954, "I wisely started with a map, and made the story fit (generally with meticulous care for distances). The other way about lands one in confusions and impossibilities, and in any case, it is weary work to compose a map from a story."[6]

Tolkien's description of his writing process, unlike other authors who might start with characters and a plot, began with the Elvish language. He then added people and genealogies, and then a map of

Middle-earth, before he finalized the story arc that would become his celebrated book. His commitment to meticulous planning led to one of the most successful novel series of all time.

Of course, Tolkien didn't have a one-year deadline, and his creative process took decades. But what matters is how he organized his work. He broke down a big idea into smaller, manageable phases. Then, he tackled them step by step.

You can do the same. Take the parts of your goal you've identified. Write down the specific steps to achieve it within a year. When you see these steps in order, even a big goal feels manageable. You can work through it one phase at a time.

The PLAN to WIN in Action

Let's walk through the steps to take your elements and write them out into the actual steps you will complete to accomplish your goal. These steps aren't difficult, but they're complex and involve several parts. For that reason, it may feel like it's a lot of work, but don't get discouraged or overwhelmed. I've broken it down so each step is easy to understand; just move through each of them one by one and take breaks if you feel overwhelmed.

Step 1: Decide What You'll Need to Succeed

Now that you've named the elements required to achieve your goal, it's time to group your brainstorm list using the PERKS acronym: People, Environment, Resources, Knowledge, and Skills. This gives you a clear view of what your goal needs. Don't worry if everything doesn't fit neatly into these categories; this step is about understanding the overall landscape.

Next, split your items into two columns: "must-haves" and "nice-to-haves." This helps you see what's necessary for progress toward achieving the goals and what will just make things smoother. For example, learning about nutrition may be a must-have for a health goal, while hiring a personal trainer could be a nice-to-have. Both are beneficial, but only one is crucial to move forward.

Finally, identify any gaps in your knowledge or skills. If your goal requires learning new skills, you can explore by watching videos, taking a class, or talking to experienced people. This step reveals what you know and what you still need to learn, helping you set realistic milestones in the next step.

Step 2: Identify and Organize Your Milestones

At this point, what you likely have is a semi-organized list of elements and potential milestones—but it isn't yet arranged in a way that's useful. This step involves identifying and organizing those milestones. However, the sequence doesn't need to be perfect, and it doesn't need to match how anyone else would approach the goal. It simply needs to make sense to you, because you're the one who will be doing the work.

The milestones required for each goal are unique because every person and every starting point is unique. Even if your goal is the same as someone else's, how quickly you can get there and what needs to happen along the way may look very different. That's why there is no universal formula for identifying milestones. Some steps will be small, such as a five-minute phone call to schedule a meeting, while others may take hours or even days. And some milestones are best measured in time, while others are better measured in outcomes, like money saved, pounds lost, miles walked, or pages read or written.

What often gets in the way here is fear and overwhelm. When people see a long list of things they think they need to do, it's easy to stall and make no progress at all. Defining and sequencing milestones helps prevent that by narrowing your focus to the next meaningful phase of work.

Some goals suggest a natural sequence. For example, if you're trying to lose weight in order to run a marathon, your first milestone might focus on building foundational habits so running feels safer and easier. Other goals, like starting a business, involve many parallel paths. You could begin with marketing, finance, legal considerations, or product development, and none of those choices would be inherently better or worse within a one-year timeframe.

For example, if your goal is to start a business within a year, your first milestone might be completing a ninety-day marketing plan. For those first three months, your focus would be limited to researching platforms, understanding your target customer, setting up accounts, and organizing ideas—nothing more. These early milestones are about education and clarity, not execution at scale. By defining and ordering your milestones this way, you lay the groundwork for an achievable PLAN to WIN and set yourself up for the next step: turning milestones into specific, actionable tasks.

For each milestone you have identified, write out the elements that are required to achieve it. Go back to your elements categories for this list and start from there. Don't worry about making a list that is in any order at first; right now, it's just a bucket to contain all the tasks you know you'll need to complete each specific milestone. After assigning each item you need to know or can do to a specific milestone, you are ready to proceed to the next step. This might also be a natural point to pause if you're feeling overwhelmed and need to take a break before continuing. There's a lot to think about and organize, so splitting the steps into smaller work sessions works really well.

Step 3: Break Your Tasks into Categories for Time Blocking

Next, you're going to take the milestone lists and start to group items into categories. For example, you might organize your tasks by subject so that all tasks related to learning go in one group, all tasks related to budgeting in another, and so on.

If a specific sequence is required for the tasks in your milestone, categorize them into ordered steps, from start to finish. For example, if you're painting a picture, you'd first need to decide what to paint, gather all your supplies, prepare them (stretching a canvas, squeezing paint onto a palette), maybe scope out places you want to work, and then go there and paint. This is a natural way to organize your tasks into steps.

But some goals may have less established processes, such as saving money. There are so many potential ways to save money that the categories you choose are less likely to be part of a sequence and instead, consist of different ways to generate more income or to save on your spending. In that situation, there isn't a wrong way to start.

Your categories might include putting aside savings from your day job, finding a side hustle, decluttering your house and selling items, coupon clipping, a tax refund, or other similar sources of income. In this example, your categories are not in any order, so you would decide what makes the most sense to you.

Step 4: Assign Your Milestones to Specific Weeks

You now have three to six milestones with tasks, organized by category. To backward plan your year, look at the entire year and decide when you want to accomplish each milestone along the way to your big goal. Take into account the things you know will happen in your life, like birthdays, vacation times, work projects, and any other event that you can predict will come up as the year goes by. This will help you plot your milestones accordingly.

Some of your milestones might take less time than others, so it isn't important to evenly space them out. And some of them might be connected to specific calendar days that aren't flexible, like the date of a half-marathon, for example, so that will give you clear places to attach them.

Although you are assigning your milestones to specific dates on your calendar, this is your starting point. The PLAN to WIN has built-in flexibility so you can move things around when life gets messy or when things don't go exactly as planned. So do your best to assign your milestones at this time, and we will just focus on the first milestone for now.

Step 5: Plan the First Week in Detail Using Time Blocking

Next, we are going to schedule your first week, and you will see the value of your organized categories. First, look at the week ahead to see what time you have available. Do you have thirty minutes on Monday, an hour after work on Thursday, and two hours on Saturday morning? The time doesn't have to be consistent in either the amount or the sequence of days; you just need to identify which chunks of time you have available this week so you can create your schedule.

Now go back to your first milestone and the organized categories you identified, and assign them to your available time chunks. Meaning, decide when you're going to invest time in reaching your milestone.

For example, if you have three main categories of tasks, you could commit to spending one hour on each category to make progress toward your goal. Or if you have four categories and only two hours you can find on your calendar, then you can give each category thirty minutes a week.

If my goal were weight loss-related, one category of activities might be meal prep, another might be strength training, and another might be low- and high-intensity cardio. Those are four categories that I'll want to schedule on my calendar throughout the week based on my availability. I might plan to do cardio three days a week and strength training on alternating days, with meal prep on weekends. Find an order that makes sense for your goal and the steps you know you need to take.

You could also designate certain days for specific activities.

For example, if your goal is to start your own business, you may decide that Monday is the day you work on finance-related tasks. Wednesday could be for legal activities, such as completing important paperwork. Friday could be for product or service-related action items. Consistently assigning categories to days of the week can help you get into a rhythm and start building momentum.

Go back through all of the time blocks you've assigned in Week 1 and write out the specific action step you will work on to make progress toward your goal. Remember that we're only looking at the first week. What from your list should be scheduled for the block of time you've set aside for your first category?

If you've set aside one hour for setting up your business on Monday, then it's time to determine what, exactly, from your task list you can do this coming Monday. Maybe one task is setting up a business bank account, which may take the whole hour since you have to go to the bank in person. That's fine, since you have sixty minutes allocated. But if you had only a thirty-minute block, you would need to go back to your master list and find a task from the business setup category that takes no more than thirty minutes and schedule that. You would need to find a sixty-minute window on another day to go to the bank.

On Wednesday, when you've designated sixty minutes for product research, you may decide that your task of researching the bestselling eBooks makes sense there. This will only take thirty minutes, so you could spend the second thirty minutes outlining some ideas for your first e-book, given what you learned about what's selling well right now.

On Fridays, you have sixty minutes set aside for social media-related work. So, using what you learned from your research on Wednesday, you could spend your hour on Friday coming up with fifty prompts or ideas for social media posts based on your e-book idea.

You're only going to assign daily tasks to the blocks you've set aside for Week 1—nothing beyond that. You're not going to plan your daily tasks for Week 2 or later until the end of Week 1, so you can adjust based on what happened in Week 1.

Assigning a specific task to a date and time makes you own it. It's a commitment now, not just wishful thinking "if you get to it." You need to protect that time and hold yourself accountable to actually do them. That way, at the end of the week, you can see what you accomplished and that you've made progress toward your goal. Remember, making all of these decisions before your week starts and creating these action step lists helps you eliminate decision fatigue so you can maintain consistent progress.

Chapter Cheat Sheet

Step 1: Decide What You'll Need to Succeed

- What do I need to clarify before I sort my messy list into clear categories?
- What can I let go of and still move forward at this time?

Step 2: Identify and Organize Your Milestones

- What four to six elements must be accomplished for my goal to be successful?
- When choosing the milestones, ask yourself: *What will have the greatest impact on achieving my goal?*

Step 3: Break tasks into categories for time-blocking

- Are the categories you originally used to organize your list transferable to time-blocking categories?
- If not, is there a more straightforward way to label them for this purpose?

Step 4: Assign your milestones to specific weeks

- What do you need to decide about your calendar and commitments before scheduling?
- What would an ideal year of work toward this goal look like on your schedule?

Step 5: Plan the first week in detail using time-blocking
- What do you need to consider before deciding which tasks belong in Week 1?
- When scheduling, how can you prioritize your natural energy levels to match the task?

Mentor Notes & Insights

Finding Balance

Often, when you schedule everything you want to do on your calendar, you'll start to see pockets of time, and realize that you have extra time here and there where you could squeeze in some tasks. For example, after the 10:00 am meeting with your client and before your 12:30 pm lunch appointment, you'll probably have at least an hour to invest in another activity. This is where you could schedule other categories from your list, and make progress toward your goal faster. But you also need to maintain a healthy balance of free time, so don't overschedule yourself; that will lead to burnout.

This is important to notice, because it may be the point at which you realize you can work on more than one goal at a time if you feel compelled to. So, as you're writing out the first goal, you'll become more aware of how much time you need to make progress on it and also how much extra time you have left over. Your life may feel hectic and overscheduled, but when you start assigning dates and times to your must-do items, you will probably find you have more free time than you think.

On the other hand, if your schedule is already jam-packed with other responsibilities, you may also come to realize that trying to pursue three goals at once is not realistic. If you're already raising teenagers, and every week you're not only working forty hours, but also exercising five hours, and volunteering five hours, most of your free time may already be spoken for if, like most humans, you also need to sleep.

What's important to realize here is that you won't know for sure what's possible and what isn't until you block out time for your categories on your calendar and commit to getting them done.

Have you seen the video of a professor demonstrating how it's possible to fit a massive bucket of stones and rocks into a glass jar? At first glance, it doesn't seem possible that what looks like three gallons of stuff can all fit into a two-gallon jar. The trick is to start with the biggest rocks. When it comes to planning, the biggest rocks in this case are your top priorities, such as work and sleep, and then you can fill in medium-sized "rocks," such as meals, exercise, spirituality, and relaxation. Once you do this, you may discover that there is still space for other things in your life, such as taking a class, reading, a hobby, or pursuing your goal, to name a few possibilities, which are the metaphorical grains of sand that go into the jar last.

So, back to your schedule. You've picked one goal, you've listed all of the tasks that will be required to achieve that goal, and you've grouped them into categories. Now you're going to schedule them on your physical calendar by writing them in. You're responsible for doing all of those things on your schedule. It's official now. And if you look at your calendar and it feels too full, then maybe you really don't have time to add a second or third goal right now. That doesn't mean you have to table them forever. It's just for now, until you've made headway on your first goal.

But you may look at your calendar and realize that what initially felt overwhelming isn't actually too bad. You know you need ninety minutes a week to reach your goal in thirteen weeks, but that doesn't mean you have to find one ninety-minute chunk. You can break it up. Maybe you only need three thirty-minute blocks of time, which you have on Monday, Wednesday, and Friday at lunch.

CHAPTER 6

I—IMPLEMENT THE PLAN

One of the most impressive stories of plan implementation is the creation of Disneyland, which Walt Disney imagined, designed, and built. In the 1940s, Disney was inspired to create an amusement park where children and adults could have fun together. The idea came to him while watching his two daughters on a merry-go-round in Los Angeles' Griffith Park. He **Pictured** an outdoor space where families could experience entertainment together and **Locked in** on the goal of creating such an amusement park.

The original plan, as he began to **Analyze** what might be possible with the resources at his disposal, was for a "Mickey Mouse Park" near the Disney Studios. The first blueprints for the park were drawn up in 1948. Not everyone was a fan of the idea, however; Disney's brother Roy expressed concern that a "fanciful, expensive amusement park would lead to financial ruin."[1]

Undeterred, Disney continued to expand and refine his vision. He **Named** the elements, which included buying land, obtaining funding, creating a story or stories to link all the park's areas, and finding construction help. He **Wrote** out the details with the help of some of Disney Studio's most talented illustrators and sold off vacation property and life insurance to raise the money needed to get started. In 1953, he hired the Stanford Research Institute to identify a possible location, leading him to purchase 160 acres of land in Anaheim. Then he and a lead designer toiled away one weekend designing the park's interior.

To get the funding needed to build the park, ABC agreed to lend Disney money in exchange for one-third ownership of Disneyland and the creation of a weekly Disney TV show. Implementation was a go, and construction began in 1954. "Mickey Mouse Park" finished in 1955, debuting a new type of immersive family entertainment venue. It was an immediate success and set a new standard for theme parks, largely due to the detailed planning at every stage and the speed with which Disney managed to implement it. Disneyland was built quickly because so much thought and planning had gone into it; executing it was probably easy.

Chapter Objective: By the end of this chapter, you will take action on your plan by completing your first week of scheduled tasks. You will track what you do each day, notice what works and what doesn't, and begin building the habits needed to follow through.

"Just Do It"

Until now, the planning steps you've been taking in the book you're holding were more cerebral, more internal work. Yes, you had to think and make decisions, but you haven't had to do much more than that. However, in this chapter, we're shifting to taking action. It's now time to implement those plans you've laid out and begin to shift from thinking about what you want and need to do to actually doing something. That's the only way you'll make progress toward achieving your goal.

Inaction is what keeps many intelligent and capable people from achieving their goals. They plan, they strategize, they research, and research, and plan, and revise, and never actually do anything. It's called analysis paralysis, and that's why they never make progress.

This system is designed to prevent that outcome.

Implementing the plan is where you tap into your initial motivation. Week 1 is where motivation is at its highest, and we really want to capitalize on that since change is hard and rewards might be farther away than we would like.

This is where that second marshmallow test is really going to happen. Can you keep progressing long enough to get the second marshmallow? Because this first week is all about the changes you have decided to make for this plan to get off the ground.

Infuse Positivity and Optimism

You're beginning your journey and taking steps toward your goal. To help you stay on track and keep your spirits high, surround yourself with positivity. You can get positive vibes from a wide range of sources, so don't feel like you necessarily need to add a new task to your workload.

Some ideas to try include putting up positive or inspiring posters or paintings on your walls, or listening to podcasts, audiobooks, or uplifting music on your commute or while you are doing chores. You could also register for free online courses or workshops on topics of interest, then listen to the audio recording while you're walking your dog. Or you could find a motivational quote that resonates with you and set it as your screensaver or wallpaper.

Your environment can help to shift your mindset. Turn on lots of lights in your space and open shades and curtains to maximize all the daylight you can get. Create an atmosphere that makes what you're trying to do seem doable. Work to boost your mood and your confidence.

Sometimes you need to tailor your plan to fit how you're feeling, because there will be days when you absolutely do not feel like doing that thing you know you need to do. Maybe you need to work out, or do some research for a project, or vacuum your floors, and you just don't want to. We've all been there.

When that happens, make a deal with yourself that the only thing you need to do is to start the task. Tell yourself that you don't have to finish it, but you at least have to start. For example, if you're supposed to go for a run, put your running shoes on and head out for five minutes. Then you can stop. However, after five minutes, you may realize you can keep going (so you do).

Sometimes Doing the Minimum is Okay

Stanford professor Kelly McGonigal, PhD, author of *The Willpower Instinct*, discusses habit formation and striving to do the bare minimum you need to do to progress toward your goal. Let's say you're trying to start a meditation practice and set a goal to meditate for an hour a day, which can be overwhelming for someone who has never meditated before. Instead of giving up entirely, McGonigal suggests trying to do just one minute a day. Do one minute a day until it seems easy, then do two minutes a day. The key, she says, isn't about the actual number or how many minutes you spend on the practice, but on doing the thing for *any* amount of time.

So, getting back to your plan for reaching your goal, it's okay if you don't do everything on the day's action plan. You may not be able to complete everything, but you have to try to do something, and that's the key to implementing the plan. You aren't implementing if you're not doing anything.

This means that, for example, even if you don't pull all the weeds in your garden, trim the front hedge, and blow the leaves off your front walkway, figure out what's the least amount you can do and still make progress toward your goal of making your front yard more attractive. Maybe today you just use the leaf blower on your front walkway. Do that, and you can call your work done for the day.

Doing that small thing will help you make progress toward your goal and keep you in action mode, which will provide some momentum to carry over into tomorrow when you may have the motivation to tackle the weeding. Don't let a day go by when you do nothing at all. At least do the bare minimum on your goal list.

My Classroom Experience

With my goals, elements, and order set, daily decisions became easier. Now that I had my plan in place, I no longer needed to start from scratch every Sunday night, figuring out the week ahead or worrying about my focus. The system helped me plan lessons, introduce new material, and review skills as the content became tougher for my students. This consistency eases decision-making and creates a calmer classroom. Students know what to expect, and I know what is important. Instead of managing chaos, I can implement a thoughtful plan designed for a real classroom.

Lisa's Journey

Future caterer Lisa noticed a big change during implementation. With a plan ready, she didn't rely on bursts of motivation or long stretches of time to get things done. Instead, she followed her structure and made steady progress in small steps. Even on days when she is exhausted, she can still refer to her plan and identify one thing she can complete to keep moving forward. Since her decisions were made, she spent less time planning and more time acting. The system provided a routine that fit her life, helping her balance work, family duties, and unexpected interruptions without halting everything.

From Idea to Reality in Record Time

Cosmetics queen Mary Kay Ash's namesake company, Mary Kay, grew out of frustration with the glass ceiling at her previous employer. After twenty-five years in direct sales, selling everything from encyclopedias to home care products to gifts, Ash, whose sales ability had reaped great rewards for her former employers, quit upon hearing that a man she had trained was being hired as her supervisor at twice her pay.[2] That was 1963. She left and planned to write a book that encapsulated all the sales lessons she had learned as her next act. However, about halfway through drafting the manuscript, she realized that she had just crafted a winning business plan for a new company.

She pivoted, taking $5,000 from her savings, and launched Beauty by Mary Kay.[3] Her **Picture** of success had evolved, and she quickly realized that what she really wanted to do was start and run a company that celebrates women and creates new opportunities for them. She **Locked in** her goal and put money down on product creation and a small, five-hundred-square-foot storefront from which she initially operated. She had received a facial cream as a gift from a leather tanner's daughter years before, which had impressed her, so Ash bought the recipe as her first product.

Analyzing her situation, she knew she needed a small group of ambitious saleswomen. She wanted to create a minimally viable operation to test things out before going all in, but she was committed to success, even when men around her tried to talk her out of it. She was ready to **Implement** only a few months later.

Having been supremely successful in direct sales, also known as in-home parties or demonstrations, Ash stuck with what worked. The women she hired were "beauty consultants," rather than salespeople, who offered in-home classes for interested women. In 1963, its first year in business, the company generated $198,000 in wholesale revenue and only grew from there.

Although Ash certainly faced times of doubt, such as when her husband died shortly before the company's planned grand opening, she moved forward nonetheless. She took **Action** rather than standing still. You can, too.

The PLAN to WIN in Action

Step 1: Set up Your Environment for Success

Setting up your environment for success might be more critical than you think. Your environment, or the people and things you surround yourself with, is essential at this stage. Your environment matters—and it matters a lot. Research by Wendy Wood, Jeffrey M. Quinn, and Deborah A. Kashy at the University of Southern California (USC) showed that 43 percent of our habits are triggered by our environment rather than by conscious choice.[4] Which means that if you set up your environment to be more conducive to the habits and behaviors you want to display in your life, you will be much more likely to succeed.

But your environment extends beyond your physical space and includes factors such as your mental and emotional states, which can make it easier or harder to reach your goal.

For example, if your goal in the next year is to write a book, there are things you can do to set yourself up for success from the outset. One is creating a space that is favorable for writing. That could mean setting up a desk or workstation at home or carving out a set time every night or every weekend specifically for writing. Think about what else you could do to make it easier for you to make progress on your book. Do you need to put your phone on "Do Not Disturb"? Do you need to print quotes from your favorite authors to use as motivation? Or maybe all you need are noise-canceling headphones.

Curate an environment and a support system that makes what you're trying to achieve easier. If you are trying to improve your fitness, and can't find a friend who wants to get up and walk with you in the morning, that's okay. Your friends and family don't have to actively participate in helping you reach your goal, but they also shouldn't get in the way or discourage you. Consider joining a local walking club or a class at a local fitness center with people who also want to get in an early morning walk.

Step 2: Follow Your Time-Blocked Plan for the First Week as Best You Can

During your first week, it's essential that you attempt to do what you have planned, even if you're not sure it will make a difference or if you feel you're not ready. Just do it. Because you know that if you don't, nothing will change, and you don't want that. That's why you took the time to create your plan in the first place.

Do what you marked on your plan as close to when you planned it as possible, to stay on track so you can begin to make progress and gain some momentum. Once you have momentum, your odds of success rise significantly.

Step 3: Keep a Simple Daily Log of Your Actions and How You Felt

Take notes or journal about what you've done each day in pursuit of your goal. Spend five minutes at the end of your day and note how you felt about what you did or didn't do, any observations you have about your behavior or your emotions, or events that triggered certain feelings. Regular journaling can help you process how you feel and document your personal growth over time. Regularly recording memorable moments, good and bad, especially as they relate to your goal, will help you make adjustments along the way to keep on track.

Step 4: Make Note of What is Working and What Isn't

As you go through your first week, it is inevitable that some of what you planned will work and some of it won't. You don't need to fix any of that this week; just make a note of it and keep trying to implement the plan you designed. Keeping a record of what went as expected and what didn't will help you set more appropriate expectations going forward. You want to be realistic with your plans, and you'll get better over time as you pay attention to your progress and any challenges that crop up.

For example, if you planned to spend thirty minutes calling to schedule some appointments on Tuesday after work, but you got pulled into a meeting unexpectedly and weren't able to make the calls before the businesses closed, make a note of it. Maybe there is a better time of day for those kinds of activities. Or maybe you planned to wake up early three days a week to walk before work. If you complete all three days, make a note of that accomplishment, as this points to it being a realistic approach to getting in your walking. If you scheduled one hour to create a project outline and finished it in thirty minutes, make a note of it. Next time, you probably don't need to allocate as much time for those kinds of activities.

An easy way to keep track of this in a physical planner is to color-code items on your list. So, for example, maybe pink is something that didn't work, yellow is something that went as planned, and green is something you finished with time left over. Find a way to make this easy for yourself; it shouldn't take more than a minute or two.

Step 5: Identify One Thing You Will Change and One Thing You Will Keep the Same for Next Week

As you conclude your first week and prepare to plan your next week, review your journal and notes and identify one thing you will keep the same and one thing you will change.

Chapter Cheat Sheet

Step 1: Set up your environment for success.

- What positivity can I surround myself with to keep my spirits high?
- What changes can I make to my environment to make it easier for me to complete today's actions?

Step 2: Follow your time-blocked plan for the first week as best you can.

- What do I need to remember about flexibility versus perfection while working on this plan?
- What can I do or say to myself to make progress, not perfection, this week?

Step 3: Keep a simple daily log of your actions and how they felt.

- Where is the best place for me to keep a simple record of my days?
- How can I set a reminder to complete this daily log?

Step 4: Notice where the plan fits your life and where it doesn't.

- What do I need to pay attention to during this first week to identify mismatches?
- How should I name exactly which parts of the plan felt easy and which felt forced?

Step 5: Identify one thing you will change and one thing you will keep the same for next week.

- When reviewing my notes, how should I prioritize what to keep or change?
- What do I need to keep track of to make Week 2 feel more aligned?

Mentor Notes & Insights

Daily Habits

Building daily habits is probably the easiest way to reach your goal. When you break your annual goal down from yearly to quarterly to monthly to weekly and then daily, the required daily task is generally very doable. It might only take a few minutes to complete, in fact. Practicing those daily habits helps build new muscles and capabilities you might never have considered.

One of my favorite examples of the power of daily habits comes from comedian Jerry Seinfeld. Seinfeld has talked about writing one joke a day; he's done so for years. Granted, he'll tell you that every joke is not necessarily a good joke. However, more importantly, he creates a chain of success. If he writes seven jokes a week and five are weak but two are really good, he's created new material he can try on an audience, which could lead to positive feedback and continued sold-out shows.

For you, Day One of your new activity may feel really hard, because you're stretching new muscles, perhaps literally. But you push through and do it. By Day Two, you know you can do it again because you just did it the day before. By Day Three, you already have two days in, and your confidence is growing. And by Day Seven, you have a week-long streak of success, it's getting easier to complete your daily task, and you're already starting to see results. Once you create this streak, you're building your own momentum. You have a track record of success that you're continuing to build. Although you haven't yet reached your goal, the streak itself is part of the goal; it's what will get you there.

CHAPTER 7

N—NAVIGATE CHALLENGES

When Susan Wojcicki took the helm of YouTube in 2014, her **Picture** of success was to make it a sustainable global platform. At the time, online video sharing was growing exponentially, and Wojcicki's biggest challenge was managing explosive growth without negatively impacting the business. She **Locked in** on a goal of building a platform that supported and protected creators and advertisers.

As she **Analyzed** the situation, she recognized the need for more corporate governance. She **Named** the elements, including systems for content moderation, creator monetization, and policy clarity, all in an effort to rein in near-out-of-control expansion. To do that, she wrote out frameworks and policies that included community guidelines, algorithm oversight, and revenue sharing with creators, and then she implemented them. She also enforced policies and monitored advertiser retention as one metric signaling success.

Unfortunately, it wasn't enough to keep platform users in line, and she found several crises she had to **Navigate**. Content moderation was one challenge that emerged quickly, and she addressed it by tightening content guidelines and hiring thousands of moderators to monitor what was being shared.[1] She also reversed declining revenue by creating new monetization strategies,[2] including beefing up YouTube's Partner Program and advertising offerings. The rise of video shorts on TikTok and Instagram created a new competitive challenge, which she successfully navigated through the rollout of YouTube Shorts.[3]

Wojcicki skillfully managed the new competitive arena by constantly shifting the online industry, referring back to documented priorities to guide her decision-making rather than making ad hoc plays. She achieved her goals and grew YouTube to the leading online video streaming platform it is today.

Chapter Objective: By the end of this chapter, you will learn how to keep going even when things don't go as planned. You will recognize the challenges that get in your way, decide what is and isn't in your control, create backup strategies for tough days, and build a weekly routine that helps you adjust your plan and keep making progress without giving up.

Checking In

The steps you take toward your goal in the first phases of implementation that we covered in the previous chapter provide insight into what is helpful and what isn't. Maybe you discover which types of actions move you forward faster than other actions you've taken. As you begin to make progress, you'll want to check in regularly and recalibrate as needed.

Using a roadmap analogy, if you're driving from Los Angeles to New York, you may find that the traffic is moving slowly on the highway and that taking the back roads will actually get you there faster. So, you adjust for at least part of the trip. Or, if speed isn't your priority and seeing all the major landmarks is, you may opt to take detours to see sights like the Grand Canyon.

As you're driving toward New York, you're going to be regularly checking your GPS or Maps app to make sure you're on the right road and that you're still headed in the right direction. These types of check-ins are likely how Wojcicki recognized the coming threats from other social media companies and was able to devise a new plan to remain competitive. When you hear about a speed check ahead, you'll slow down, just like when you hear there may be a hazard in the road. You pay attention, and you adjust your course. That's part of the checking in and recalibrating that planning requires.

Continuous Improvement

Planning for goal achievement is a continuous improvement process. That means you set a goal, create a detailed plan to get there, and implement the plan. But once you get started, you may realize there is more to do than you thought or that new information has made something easier for you, so you adapt and recalibrate.

For example, if you're starting a new business, you may find this to be true: What you initially put your efforts into might not be what your customers are most interested in, so you adapt to meet their needs. Or if you achieve the goal of buying a home, and then decide to expand your family with a child or a dog, you may realize that the home no longer fits your needs, so you sell it to buy something else. You'll rarely reach your goal and be satisfied for the rest of your life with where you ended up. Most people continue to strive to achieve more or something different.

Sometimes during the implementation stage, your priorities, circumstances, or perspective change. Or maybe you see that your original goal was a step toward a much larger goal you were initially too afraid to shoot for. It's that bigger goal that you're headed toward now, but you had to start somewhere. That's why I call it a continuous improvement plan. You have a goal. You have to take the first step. But that goal will redefine itself as you grow personally and your life evolves.

Planning is a flexible process; it's not rigid. Rigidity leads to burnout, whereas a strong plan adjusts with you. Planning *requires* failure along the way, so that you can learn what works and what doesn't for you. You can't do that until and unless something goes wrong somewhere.

Problems are a given. No matter how well you plan, challenges will crop up. Some level of revision of your original plan is inevitable. Events and circumstances may arise that interfere with your progress toward your goal. Despite these barriers, some minor and some major, your mindset will help keep you on track. The healthier and more optimistic your mindset, the more committed you'll be to reaching your objective and the less likely you'll give up when you face a challenge.

Although many factors can get in the way of you reaching your goal, the biggest roadblock I have observed is mindset. I suspect that at least 50 percent of the reasons people don't continue pursuing their goals are rooted in mindset. They get flustered, overwhelmed, distracted, and things go off-course, and then they begin to wonder if they should give up because they're so far behind.

Life is dynamic. People get sick, cars break down, schedules change, motivation fluctuates, and we have to adapt and adjust. Planning won't eliminate the chaos; it just prepares you for it and builds in flexibility. You're not planning for perfection; you're planning for the reality of everyday life.

Revision also does not mean you failed; it only means that some part of your plan needed to change. Sometimes the change comes from within you, and sometimes it is entirely external. You just have to roll with it. Changing a plan is a sign of growth because it shows that you can adjust when the path you are on isn't working anymore.

Rather than stubbornly trying to fit that round peg in the square hole, you find ways to maneuver, navigate, and make progress despite unexpected events.

My Classroom Experience

No academic year goes as planned, and the PLAN to WIN system reflects that. I can expect sudden schedule changes, student absences, dips in motivation, and external pressures. When these happen, I don't react emotionally or abandon the plan. Instead, I use the system to stay on track.

With clear goals and steps, I can adjust without losing focus. I know which parts of the plan are flexible and which aren't. This understanding helps me respond thoughtfully rather than impulsively. The outcome isn't a perfect year, but a manageable one. Progress continues despite obstacles, and more students are ready for the exam because the system adapts rather than collapses.

Lisa's Journey

When life got busy—full weeks at school, family duties, or self-doubt—Lisa-the-future-caterer kept pushing toward her goal. She adjusted her system as needed when weeks became overscheduled. With a clear goal and organized steps, she knew when to pause and when to keep moving. Her plan handled disruptions well. In the end, bouncing back mattered more than having one super productive week. Lisa made progress in her business and proved to herself that she could follow through, even when things weren't perfect.

Zigging and Zagging with Technology Disruption

One of the best stories of success in navigating challenges is Reed Hastings, cofounder of Netflix. You may recall that years ago, Blockbuster retail stores were the only place to rent new movies. Hastings recognized the inconvenience of having to travel to pick up DVDs, so he and his partners created a service that let people select movies they wanted to watch on its website and have them delivered by mail. Hastings **Pictured** a service entertainment company and **Locked in** on providing entertainment by mail, which no one else was doing on a grand scale.

He **Analyzed** what the company needed to succeed and then **Named** the elements, which included a technology infrastructure to facilitate all rental transactions. However, as he was building the infrastructure, he saw that the future wasn't in physical disks but in online streaming straight to TVs. He modified his business plan to transition Netflix from physical DVDs to an online streaming service; "Our big obsession was streaming,"[4] he said in 2011. He monitored streaming adoption rates as a metric of success.

Netflix rolled out streaming as a separate option for accessing movies and an alternative to DVD rentals. Unfortunately, his brilliant idea to split the two services was almost his downfall. He rebranded the DVD side of the business as Qwikster and effectively raised the total cost for customers who wanted both physical DVDs and streaming by 60 percent.[5] The price jump that accompanied the new combination led customers to leave in droves. Netflix's market share plummeted.

Quickly realizing his mistake, Hastings backtracked and did what few entrepreneurs do—he apologized, shut down Qwikster, and started exploring how to provide customers with original content they couldn't find elsewhere.[6] That's how *House of Cards* came to be. The success of that series propelled Netflix to become the number one streaming service worldwide today. Not only did that move differentiate Netflix at a time when other streaming services had debuted, but it also provided an alternative to rising movie licensing costs.

Hastings' plan was successful because he encountered challenges, made decisions, then admitted his mistake, recalibrated his growth plan, and moved forward.

<u>The PLAN to WIN in Action</u>

When bracing for challenges, here are steps to address and get past them.

Step 1: Identify the Most Common Disruptions or Obstacles that Arose in Your First Week

Adjustments might be as simple as extending your deadline after you start implementing your plan and realize you haven't given yourself enough time. Or maybe you realize you left out some steps that need to be taken early on, so you give yourself some time to complete them.

You learn as you go. When you created your plan, you didn't know everything you do now, even after a few days. So, you modify it.

Maybe your big goal is to lose ninety pounds, and your first milestone is to lose forty pounds in thirteen weeks. A week in, you may realize that's probably not doable given your current lifestyle. Your big goal remains the same, but you change your first milestone to thirty pounds to make it more realistic.

Or maybe you discover that the time you blocked off to work on your goal doesn't work with your biorhythms. If you're a morning person but you set aside an hour after dinner to practice the piano, that timeframe may not be ideal for you, but you wouldn't have discovered this until you began executing on your plan. And the fix is easy—change when you practice to the morning, before work. You'll have less resistance to completing tasks if you align them with when you are higher energy. Adjust your plan.

In another example, you could find that you're having trouble fitting an hour's worth of work into your plan, despite blocking off sixty minutes three times a week. You just can't seem to keep that time protected, or maybe you don't have the energy to work for an hour straight. Your adjustment could be to split those sixty-minute blocks into two thirty-minute windows. You adjust your plan to fit your current reality.

Or you could discover that your goal may have been too ambitious, given your schedule, and you haven't been able to follow through as you'd hoped. If your goal is to write a book, instead of trying to write five times a week, scale it back to two times a week or only on weekends. Then, once you're consistent, try to add another block of writing and build from there. Figure out what's actually going to work for you.

What's happening here is that you're potentially reducing or increasing the size of the milestone or the pace at which you're working, or even when you complete your work, but you're not abandoning your plan or your goal.

Step 2: Determine Which Obstacles are Controllable, Influenceable, or Outside Your Control

It's very likely that as you start taking action on your plan, you may find that you're not making the progress you had expected or hoped for. You may need to adjust your plan, but before you can do that, you need to evaluate what's getting in the way of your progress.

The knee-jerk reaction for some people is to blame the outside world for their lack of progress. It's the weather, it's the economy, it's your kids or your spouse, or your car, or the company you usually buy from. But as you probably already know, external factors are generally not the source of the problem. In most cases, the holdup is internal.

To figure out your problem, look at what you have tracked versus what you had planned, such as comparing your budget to your actual spending. Take a close look at your actions and where things went awry.

You can only uncover what's getting in your way by collecting data and analyzing the facts. You need to continue to conduct honest self-assessments like you did in chapter 3, "Analyzing Your Starting

Point." What worked and what didn't? Why could that be? What else was going on? Why did you not do what you had planned?

As a teacher looking at the situation, I liken it to a struggling student. I wouldn't tell them, "Try harder." That's not helpful at all. They could be trying their absolute best and not getting the outcome they want. Instead, we need to diagnose the obstacle. Is it that they don't understand the directions? Do they not have the skill to follow the directions? Is it that the assignment itself is poorly written and needs revision? Do they have an emotional resistance to completing the task? When we talk through all the potential issues, the student and I can diagnose what's going on and adjust the plan.

It's the same thing in real life. If you're not willing to investigate to figure out why, exactly, you have not completed your planned tasks this week, then how could you make revisions to the plan? You don't know what to change because you don't know what caused your failure this week. I suspect a big part of the problem is that people have a hard time accepting that sometimes they are the problem, and people often resist owning up to that.

Let's be clear, however: None of this is a sign of failure. When you learn more about yourself, you can adjust your plan to help you succeed. You just need to appreciate who and what you are. Maybe you always thought you were a night owl, but actually, you're a morning person. Maybe you always thought you were bad with money, but it turns out you just weren't taught some of the basics of personal finance. Maybe you thought you were a slow learner, only to discover you're not slow, but you are an auditory learner, while most classes are designed for visual learners.

To get to the heart of what's stopping you, you need to be willing to hear hard truths and then to take action to eliminate those obstacles. Those actions may be easier or more complicated than you expect, but it is definitely possible to make these necessary changes.

Step 3: Develop "Plan B" and "Low-Energy" Versions of Your Key Actions for Challenging Days

You are much more likely to falter on days when you just aren't feeling it. These low-energy days may be days when you have no energy for anything, or maybe it's that you have no energy for your planned action toward your goal.

To get past these days or prevent them from recurring, consider your typical patterns of behavior. Why do you think you feel this way? Are there emotional triggers you need to explore? What do you need to recognize and understand about yourself and these tendencies for stressful or low-energy days?

It can also be helpful to explore what success would look like if you always had a smaller, easier version of your planned activity ready. These would be step-downs from what you were supposed to do.

For example, if you overdid it with exercise over the weekend and are now in pain, it's unlikely you'll want to go for that thirty-minute run today. So, what's your plan B—your fallback? It can't be "do nothing." That won't allow you to make progress toward your goal. So, what's a reasonable, less strenuous win? Maybe a slow walk to stretch out your muscles? Or lifting weights? Or even a short swim?

Come up with several potential plan Bs so that you never have to think hard about what to do when these types of situations come up.

Step 4: Establish a Simple Weekly Review Ritual to Adjust Your Plan (Not Abandon It)

Once you figure out what's getting in your way of making progress, it's time to make the changes and then build on them. You want to make progress, but not move so quickly that you hurt yourself or sabotage the plan entirely.

For example, in our running scenario, if your goal is to run a marathon and you haven't run in a while, you're going to work up to running long distances. You may start by walking around the block, then walking half a mile, then a mile. You're adding more distance as your stamina increases. Then you start jogging a mile, then running a mile, then running three miles, five miles, and so on, until you can run 26.2 miles.

With progression planning, you're building up to achieving your goal through smaller steps. It's like building Lego structures. If you bought the Lego Icons Eiffel Tower set, with 10,001 pieces, as your first Lego project, you're likely to become very frustrated very quickly. You may even decide to give up; it's so huge and so hard to construct. A better approach would be to buy a smaller Lego kit, to get used to the pieces and how they fit together. Once that one's done, you can buy a bigger kit with more pieces, followed by an even bigger one. You keep increasing the challenge as your skills develop. You adjust along the way so that you continue to skill-build and succeed.

When you try to do too much at once, you can get lost in confusion if you move too fast. It would be like enrolling a third-grader in a calculus class. They're simply not ready. But through progression planning, you build on one thing after another.

If you're introducing a behavior change, it might be writing once a week for ten minutes until it's relatively easy and you can do it without much effort. Then maybe you progress to writing for twenty minutes a week, and you do that until it's almost second nature or you feel you've mastered it. You might even find yourself writing for more than twenty minutes naturally. That's when you know it's time to bump up your writing time to thirty minutes a week. You want to learn new skills or introduce new behaviors and work up to mastery.

Step 5: Define "Continuing Forward" When Things Go Wrong—Your Personal Minimal Viable Progress (MVP)

I've discovered over time that there are three major pitfalls in planning: loss of motivation, disruption or life events, and negative self-talk or mindset. Each of these, individually or together, can take you off course, so the best way to prevent that is to revisit what to do when they crop up.

We all lose motivation from time to time. It's going to happen. Fortunately, if you have a plan, you can make progress even when you're not particularly motivated. There are many days when I am exhausted or the end of the school year seems so far away, and I feel discouraged when I walk into my classroom. But because I already have a plan, I just need to follow the steps I've written for the day. Sometimes going through the steps changes my energy, and I start to build momentum. Sometimes I just go through the motions. Either way, the plan moves forward, and I made progress. So, when you lack motivation, just keep doing the task you had planned to do. Keep pushing ahead by pushing past the urge to do nothing.

With any life disruption, the best approach is to pause and then reset. Don't ever give up, just pause to deal with what's going on and then reset. By reset, I mean picking up where you left off or even revising your goal to reflect your new reality. Maybe you got a new job with very different hours. You may need to adjust when you work on your goal, but you're not going to completely give up on pursuing it. But as you're working through the disruption, do at least a minimal amount to stay on course.

For example, if your goal is to lose weight and you can't exercise for a couple of weeks because you broke your foot, don't give up on your weight-loss goal; just find other ways to support it. Maybe you adjust your caloric intake, or you pick up weights to build upper-body strength. And maybe your new goal during this period of recovery is not to regain any weight. Ideally, you pause so your foot can heal, but you don't backslide into bad habits.

Breaking negative self-talk or a negative mindset can happen if you train yourself to flip the negative into a positive. When your brain is mired in negative thinking, you may think, "What if this happens?" and the response is a negative outcome.

For example, "What if I rent a car and I get into an accident on my trip up the coast that I've been planning for months?" Try to become aware of this tendency toward negative thoughts and then challenge the negative assumption. Even better, take it a step further and look at potential positive outcomes. Starting by asking, "What if everything goes smoothly?" Imagine driving up the coast in a car without incident, where you didn't have to put miles on your own car, and you could rent a convertible to enjoy the ocean breeze on your trip.

The trick is to break yourself of the habit of automatically assuming a negative outcome. If you can do that, and then replace it with a positive outcome, it will be easier to imagine yourself achieving your goal. It will help keep you motivated to make progress because you know it is realistic to pursue your goal.

A big part of avoiding these pitfalls comes down to self-awareness. You previously reviewed your strengths, weaknesses, opportunities, and threats to be more cognizant of where you're tripping yourself up. You have to learn to recognize when you are the problem. The good news is that you control how you behave, which is easier to address than something beyond your control.

So, if you stop to analyze why you're not making progress, you have to look at what actually happened and take ownership of why it didn't. Because if you keep going and repeat the same mistakes over and over again, you'll get nowhere, and you may become super frustrated. Continuing to practice self-awareness will help.

Goal achievement is not a single event; it is an ongoing process that requires action, evaluation, and revision.

As we've discussed, you may also outgrow your original plan. Sometimes, as you're working through your planning process, you may realize that your original goal was actually different from what you wrote down. Maybe you couldn't articulate it as clearly at the outset, and now that you've made some progress, you can.

This often becomes clear if your plan feels too easy. Maybe you gave yourself too much time to reach your goal; maybe you underestimated your abilities, and you need to expand your goal or shorten your deadline because you're making such great progress. It doesn't make sense to take a whole year to get it done.

On the other hand, if you experience major life events that affect the pursuit of your goal, give yourself grace. You're not a failure if you haven't made progress since a family member died, you lost your job, or suddenly had to find new housing. The stress from major life changes will affect your ability to function mentally and emotionally, and your energy and attention should be focused on those situations for the moment.

I'm not saying you should completely abandon your goal in those situations, though; instead, it's more of a pause. You can scale back your progress, but having something that remains constant in your routine can actually be healthy. Sticking with even part of your plan can provide a sense of control over one part of your life, even if other things are temporarily going off the rails.

Scaling back might mean reducing how often you do something each week, such as working out, volunteering, or working on your side hustle. Don't abandon it entirely; make space to process the parts of your life that are in chaos right now. You can ramp back up when things settle down.

Starting over is rarely the solution, unless your goal is no longer aligned with your values, or if your plan was built on a faulty assumption. Maybe you've been working on saving for a home, and you receive a buyout at work that immediately funds that goal. Or maybe you've been studying French because you were planning a trip to Paris next year, and now you've pivoted and decided to go to Spain for an event. You can start studying Spanish instead, but the bigger goal here wasn't necessarily to become fluent in French; it was to prepare for a big trip, and you're still doing that. But you didn't start over; you just revised your plan.

Remember your anchor—the reason you set your goal in the first place.

Chapter Cheat Sheet

Step 1: Identify the most common disruptions or obstacles that arose in your first few weeks.

- What do I need to review (calendar, log, memories) to accurately list my real-world obstacles?
- What are the patterns that seem to consistently throw me off?

Step 2: Determine which obstacles are controllable, influenceable, or outside your control.

- What do I need to clarify before categorizing obstacles into these three groups?
- What if I stopped fighting what I can't control and focused on what I can?

Step 3: Develop "plan B" and "low-energy" versions of your key actions for challenging days.

- What do I need to accept about my own tendencies on stressful or low-energy days?
- What if I always had a smaller, easier version of my plan ready?

Step 4: Establish a simple weekly review ritual to adjust your plan (not abandon it).

- What do I need to decide about when and how I'll conduct a weekly review?
- What if my weekly review became a non-negotiable reset point?

Step 5: Define "continuing forward" when things go wrong— your personal Minimal Viable Progress (MVP) rule.

- What beliefs do I need to establish about progress and perfection before I set my MVP rule?
- What if, no matter what happened, I always did something that moved me forward?

Mentor Notes & Insights

The Role Mindfulness Plays

As you navigate your plan and become aware of what it will take to reach your goal, remember to pause before reacting to challenges. Instead, stop to check in with yourself to confirm that your intentions and actions are aligned. Pause and reflect regularly, such as weekly or monthly, as you revise your plan to confirm you're still on a path that feels right to you.

You need to pay mindful attention to the plan to achieve your goals. When you pause to reflect on your plan, you increase your chances of success by focusing on what you want to happen in your life. Mindfulness helps retrain your brain to respond rather than react to the world around you. This will help you reduce stress and regulate your emotions, moving you forward toward your goal. If you pause and think about all the steps you've planned out and remember the anchor for what you want to do, whatever it is you're doing, you're already a big step ahead of the vast majority of people who are not reflecting at all on their lives.

CASE STUDIES

To help you understand how to apply what you've just learned about The PLAN to WIN, I want to share some case studies with you. These will explain how the framework can help you break down a larger goal and make consistent progress toward achieving it.

The four case studies I'll be sharing are using the plan to:

- Start a business
- Lose weight
- Write a nonfiction book
- Create an online course

Although the goals differ, the process is the same.

USING THE PLAN TO WIN TO START A BUSINESS

Chapter Objective: By the end of this chapter, you will be able to identify the key components of starting a business from scratch. You will see how I launched my own business by moving from "thinking about starting a business" to creating a launch strategy and building a functioning business with paying clients within a year.

What This Case Study Shows:
- You can move from thinking about starting a business to establishing it.
- You don't need to be "ready" before launching.
- You can develop your offer based on your skills and interests.
- You need resilience built into your plan to get past early

challenges.

- The PLAN to WIN system works because it breaks the process of starting a business into clear, manageable steps, prioritizes action over perfection, and builds in checkpoints to evaluate progress, refine business offerings, and respond strategically to obstacles.

If you've ever thought about starting your own business, you're in the majority. According to the Shopify-Gallup Entrepreneurship Study, 62 percent of Americans would rather be their own boss than an employee.[1] The top reasons for starting a business include the opportunity to earn more money, have a more flexible schedule, and pursue a passion project. However, when it comes to taking financial risks, the numbers drop: 49 percent of aspiring entrepreneurs say they aren't willing to risk much, if any, money at all.

Still, the number of new entrepreneurs continues to rise. As of 2024, the U.S. Small Business Administration's Office of Advocacy reported that there were more than 36.2 million small businesses in the U.S. and that nine out of every ten new jobs created were by new ventures.[2]

You may be surprised to learn that 99.9 percent of all U.S. businesses are considered small businesses because they have fewer than five hundred employees. Small businesses are the economic engine that powers the country. You're smart to consider starting your own business, whether you test it out first as a side hustle or go all in from the start.

Despite the millions of new businesses started each year, many more never get off the ground. Numerous aspiring entrepreneurs get tripped up by their planning process. That is, they think they need to know everything there is to know about their business before jumping in, so they continue to research and investigate, gathering information rather than starting and adjusting as they learn. Others don't want to move forward until everything is perfectly set up.

Sometimes the problem is spending too much time on the preparation, delaying the grand opening, when minimal systems are often all you need to get started.

You do not have to have it all figured out before you take the leap; you really just need a plan that you commit to following.

Like many adults, I dreamed for years about starting my own business. With a diverse set of skills and interests, I have never been able to narrow it down to what that business would be. The PLAN to WIN system helped me make that decision and finally launch my own business. This chapter is designed to help you do the same: start and build a business that is ready to serve paying clients within a year. It's not a masterclass in marketing, branding, or scaling, only in planning the startup process.

To get your company up and running in the next year, follow The PLAN to WIN to map out all the steps you'll take to get there. Here's how I did it.

P—Picture Your Success

After decades in teaching, I realized that retirement was around the corner and that I'd need to keep working to stay active and generate a little income once I stopped teaching. I had to visualize what retirement would look like for me. Where did I want to work? What did I want to do?

When I pictured what a successful retirement looked like to me, I saw immediately that I was in charge. I didn't work for anyone else—I was a business owner. I could see it clearly. I controlled my schedule, who I worked for, and what projects I took on. My days were flexible, and I was happy and engaged in my work. I felt proud to have my own business. My life was happy and had minimal stress—only the good kind that gives you energy and motivation.

It was very clear that my goal was to start a business, but what kind of business should I start? I have a diverse set of skills and interests, so I needed to **Lock in** on one business goal.

L—Lock In On One Goal

After years of dabbling in online research and becoming fascinated with health, wellness, and longevity, I enrolled in the Headspace Health Coach program to become a certified health coach.

I didn't really have a long-term plan for this program at the outset. I'm a lifelong learner, and I love to learn new things all the time. I've always been like this. I quickly realized I could start an actual health-coaching business as a side hustle.

I locked in to create a plan to launch my new health-coaching side hustle so that once I had completed the certification program, I would be able to use this new qualification to generate revenue.

The first step was to define what that business would look like. I needed a clear goal for what to do with this new Health Coaching Certification once I completed it, so that it could serve as the basis for a new business.

With this general sense of what I wanted my health coaching business to be, I started zeroing in on how to make it a reality.

Instead of writing "start a business" as my target objective, I set a SMART (Specific, Measurable, Achievable, Relevant, Timebound) goal, which was:

- Specific: A functioning health coaching business
- Measurable: At least one paying client
- Achievable: Starting as a side hustle makes it more realistic
- Relevant: Provides a means of using the Health Coaching Certification
- Time-bound: One year

I summarized this as: "By this time next year, I will have a functioning health coaching business, with a detailed service package, legal setup, online presence, and at least one paying client."

This statement helped clarify what success looked like, so that I could then work backwards from that point to make it a reality.

A—Analyze Your Starting Point

Before I could move forward with planning my business, I needed to be honest about where I was starting from. So, I completed an AWARE scan to analyze my starting point. I needed to get clear on where I was in relation to where I wanted to be.

As with most new initiatives, you never know what you don't know, which, it turns out, was a very long list. I couldn't have predicted how much was still unknown to me, because it was only when I started making progress that the next steps became clear.

The AWARE Scan: Starting a Business

A—Arrive in the Moment

My weekdays are consumed by teaching, grading, and student needs, leaving me drained by the end of the school day. Lately, I've devoted my time and energy to school responsibilities and recovering from my workday, not planning my business. I'm most productive in the early morning, but I often put off progress, thinking I need more time and energy than I actually do.

W—Witness Without Judgment

When I think about taking a small step toward my health coaching business, I'm flooded with thoughts of being too tired or not ready. Right before I procrastinate, I feel mentally exhausted and tell myself it'll be easier during a school break. A neutral observer would say I've been gathering ideas this week, but I haven't taken any visible action.

A—Allow What Is

I have non-negotiable constraints, such as a full teaching schedule, limited weekday energy, and the need for rest. I also have self-imposed constraints, such as perfectionism and the belief that progress requires large chunks of time. On tough days, the smallest action I can allow is five minutes of writing or planning.

R—Root Yourself

Friends would describe me as consistent, empathetic, and reliable. My difficult habit loop is exhaustion leading to avoidance and short-term relief. By replacing avoidance with a brief, low-effort action, I get the same relief while building momentum.

E—Engage Mindfully

My five-minute version of progress is writing one sentence or sending one message related to my business. When I say "done for today," it means I've taken one visible action and recorded it. When resistance or overwhelm shows up, I'll pause, start small, and review my progress weekly to adjust rather than quit.

I also did a SWOT analysis (strengths, weaknesses, opportunities, and threats):

SWOT Analysis: Starting a Health Coaching Business

Strengths

- A strong foundation in health knowledge, backed by a formal health coaching credential
- Credibility built from prior teaching and coaching experience
- A personal health journey that fosters authentic connections with future clients
- A genuine passion to help others improve their health, driven by intrinsic motivation

Weaknesses

- No established audience or email list, with limited knowledge of how to build or utilize one
- Limited business and marketing experience, especially in online environments
- No consistent social media presence
- An emerging professional identity, still strongly tied to being

a teacher rather than a health coach

Opportunities
- A growing demand for midlife health coaching, particularly among women seeking practical and sustainable approaches
- Access to free online courses, tools, and business education to bridge knowledge gaps
- Availability of some financial resources for required startup costs, such as a website and basic marketing
- The ability to leverage teaching skills to create clear, structured, and educational coaching offers

Threats
- A crowded wellness and coaching market, making differentiation crucial
- Limited weekly capacity (six to eight hours), requiring careful prioritization and focus
- The risk of burnout from balancing full-time teaching with business startup demands
- Self-doubt and comparison are fueled by highly visible, more established online coaches

This analysis helped me pinpoint my focus for Year One and really understand my starting point. With so many tasks involved in starting a business, it's easy to feel overwhelmed. Being aware of these factors helps set realistic boundaries for what can be accomplished in the first twelve months.

N—Name the Elements

I listed as many elements as I could think of that would help my business thrive and be a positive force in my life. This included:
- Creating a business name, website, and email address
- Having a minimum of one paying client within a year

- Creating a simple, structured coaching program
- Outlining a course for asynchronous coaching
- Shifting my identity from "I'm thinking about health coaching" to "I am a health coach"
- Working six to eight hours per week on creating the business

Feeling calm, organized, and confident when discussing my business

W—Write It Out

In reviewing my list of tasks to be completed to achieve my goal, I organized them into five categories (PERKS): people, environment, resources, knowledge, and skills. Each category represents a type of resource or piece of information I would need:

People

- Accountant, bookkeeper, or software to track all cash flow
- Attorney
- Business insurance agent
- Mentor or accountability partner

Environment

- Dedicated weekly CEO work block scheduled
- Organized digital storage for client files

Resources

- Squarespace with Stripe for payment processing
- HIPAA-compliant video platform
- Scheduling tool

Knowledge

- How to structure a coaching program
- Basic legal and financial requirements of starting and running a business

Skills
- Running discovery calls to persuade clients to hire me
- Guiding client behavior change once they are in my program
- Writing client-facing materials to attract and keep clients

I also identified four non-negotiables I would need to establish to get started and be successful:
- A clearly defined coaching offer
- A compliant payment process
- A simple onboarding system
- A weekly block to run and build the business

After reflecting on my long list of requirements to start my business, it became clear that, beyond these four non-negotiables, everything else was optional until after I officially launched. When it came right down to it, I needed something to sell customers, a way to process their payments, and add them to my internal coaching system, and the time set aside to provide the services I had sold. That was it.

Using the categories I just created, I divided the tasks to be completed into four quarters, keeping in mind the prerequisites for some. For example, I couldn't set up my business bank account until I had finished the paperwork for my business name and had an IRS employee identification number (EIN), which is like a Social Security number for businesses. These bureaucratic delays and challenges were very frustrating, and not knowing what I didn't know was also a significant challenge at this stage. But I got started and wrote out what I could and then added to it as I learned along the way.

The four-phase, twelve-month plan looked like this:

Quarter 1
- Narrow my niche and health coaching promise
- Write a one-sentence value/mission statement
- Have conversations with friends and family to validate ideas
- Choose a business name
- Start looking for website hosts and URL availability

Milestone: Clear business concept identified and selected

Quarter 2
- Build a twelve-week coaching program framework
- Start creating the materials for the program, including:
    o Client intake form
    o Coaching agreement
    o Process diagram
- Choose pricing
- Register business as a sole proprietorship; register a DBA with the county
- Open a business bank account

Milestones: Service ready to deliver/ Graduate coaching program

Quarter 3
- Create website
- Choose a payment processing platform
- Set up a bookkeeping system to track expenses and income
- Find a HIPAA-compliant client system
- Finish creating the materials for the program, including:
    o Client intake form
    o Coaching agreement
    o Process diagram

Milestone: Fully operational backend

Quarter 4
- Announce business to personal network
- Run three free beta sessions with friends
- Collect one testimonial
- Sign the first paying client

Milestone: Business is live and serving clients

With this initial framework for the first year completed, I planned out my first week, day by day, and made decisions to ensure my success. I plotted these action items on my physical calendar and set alarms on my phone as reminders. Because I was so specific, I only had to follow the plan.

I—Implement the Plan

As a full-time teacher, I couldn't work on the business full-time. To allow for solid progress in the time I did have, I chose to schedule one ninety-minute to two-hour block each week to work on each of the following:

- Planning
- Client prep
- Messaging and outreach
- Administrative tasks

I always followed the Minimal Viable Progress (MVP) Rule:

If I couldn't complete a full task or didn't have the larger time chunk available, I did a smaller version. For example, if I couldn't write a whole blog post or email, I wrote an outline of my thoughts to complete later. If writing the copy or building an entire webpage was too much, I just wrote the copy and planned to build later.

The goal is not perfection but consistent progress through even the tiniest regular action.

N—Navigate Challenges

Knowing that there would be roadblocks and problems along the way, I tried to be proactive by identifying the most likely barriers. For me, these were:

- Challenge: Fear of being seen online → Reset Strategy: Don't try to do everything or be everywhere at once. Choose one platform and try photos first before videos.
- Challenge: Difficulty describing my offer → Reset Strategy: Practice with friends, but also know that perfection isn't possible or necessary.

- Challenge: Increased workload during busy cycles → Reset Strategy: Lean on outside resources to supplement my own work capacity.
- Challenge: Information Overload → Reset Strategy: Mindfulness meditation sessions + do a jigsaw puzzle to wind down.

I knew that those wouldn't be my only challenges and that I didn't know what might happen, so I prepared for the unexpected by creating a toolbox of four steps to refocus when those things happened:

- Return to my one-year outcome picture.
- Identify one action I can control.
- Reduce the task if necessary, but do not abandon it.
- Review progress weekly, not during emotional spikes.

For example, some of the obvious workarounds were:

- If I skip a Monday email, I will send one out before the weekends.
- If I doubt my expertise, I will review comments from my coaching program mentors to reinforce my identity.
- When I was setting up my business, I realized there were many steps I didn't know about, so I adjusted the plan to include the new information as I learned it.

And then I got to work.

What Actually Happened

By following the PLAN to WIN process, I hit the following milestones:

- Quarter 1: I chose my niche, business name, and core promise.
- Quarter 2: I built a twelve-week coaching framework, and graduated from the certification program.
- Quarter 3: I registered my business, opened a business account, and set up payment and client documents.
- Quarter 4: I announced business, ran a beta program, and

signed two paying clients.

At the end of twelve months, I had achieved the target milestones I had set and had a business. Interestingly, it wasn't what I had pictured.

As I navigated through the challenges, I learned about myself and the kind of work I wanted to do, and ended up deciding to go in a completely different direction. As I applied my own system, I realized my true passion wasn't coaching others on health, but coaching people on planning for goal achievement. I made the conscious decision to pivot and become the author of the very book you're reading. Building this business revealed a truer, more aligned goal for me. I realized that hustling to help people one-on-one make healthier choices limited both my reach and the scope of my impact.

I truly believe that this experience was life-changing, and although the destination wasn't what I expected, I learned so much along the way. The system didn't fail; it succeeded in revealing my true objective, which is the ultimate form of winning. Writing this book allowed me to share a flexible system for change, one that can be used to achieve far more than health goals and reach many more in the process.

Every meaningful transformation is simply:

Picture → Lock In → Analyze → Name → Write → Implement → Navigate

That is how you win.

CHAPTER 9

Health isn't built by intensity. It's built by consistency.
—Dr. Stacy Sims

USING THE PLAN TO WIN TO LOSE WEIGHT

Chapter Objective: By the end of this chapter, you will be able to identify the key components of an effective plan to achieve better health, including a clear health destination, a measurable goal, tracking metrics, and strategies for managing barriers and enablers.

What This Case Study Shows:
- Big goals become manageable when broken into layers of twelve-months, ninety-days, weekly, and daily.
- Success comes from predictable follow-through, not perfection.
- Identity-based planning ("I am someone who…") is far more effective than punishment-based planning ("I have been bad, so now I must try harder").
- The PLAN to WIN system works for this goal because it

reflects how learning and changing behaviors happen: through a continuous improvement plan with cycles of planning, action, reflection, and adjustment.

At the end of 2024, 55 percent of Americans wanted to lose weight, according to Gallup's Annual Health and Healthcare Survey.[1] The percentage of people who believe they are overweight has continued to climb, with 43 percent feeling that way at the end of 2024, so it's no surprise that there are so many people interested in slimming down or getting healthier.

Although New Year's is probably the most common time for people to set new resolutions or intentions, those goals rarely stick. In fact, 80 percent of people who set those goals on January 1 give them up by February, just a few weeks later.[2]

The problem isn't a lack of commitment; it's a lack of a plan to follow when life gets in the way. Many people think that willpower or pure determination will make it possible for them to shed the pounds. (Hint: It won't.)

They also try to do too many things at once, like starting a diet, a new exercise program, *and* cutting back on desserts. It's often all or nothing, and they give up entirely after a single bad day. That makes it even harder to stick with a plan to cut calories or eat more protein.

The following case study shows you how to set and achieve weight-loss goals.

In July of 2024, I turned fifty, and I realized my health was not where I wanted it to be. This milestone birthday was the catalyst for that change. So, I set out to make a PLAN to WIN for health coaching, and I became my own first client. Here's what I did.

P—Picture Your Success

I knew I wanted to get healthier, but first I had to figure out what that even meant to me. I started by thinking about my life in the larger sense—turning fifty will do that to you! I envisioned being sixty, seventy, eighty-plus years old, and began paying attention to anyone around me who seemed to be that age, noticing what they could or couldn't do in regard to mobility—getting around easily, standing up or sitting down—and their cognitive abilities—how sharp were they? Becoming more aware of what is possible at various ages helped me start to imagine what I wanted for myself.

Like many of you, I'm a busy woman. I can't spend all day at the gym or hire a personal chef to cook my healthy meals. I'm a fifty-year-old teacher and dog mom with a busy social life. I'm also a realist. I'm not trying to become a fitness influencer; I just want to feel strong, healthy, and confident. Looking ahead, I want to be independent and able to move, to enjoy life. I want to be able to clean my house or do my grocery shopping without assistance. I want to get up every morning without an achy body, etc.

This led me to the picture of what being healthier would look like a year later, at fifty-one.

The image I conjured was a detailed picture of my next birthday.

That took the form of a "one-year-from-now" reflection written in the present tense, as if it were a year later and I'd already achieved my goal. Mine looked like this:

"It is July, 2025. I sleep deeply through the night, and in the morning, I feel energized. I wake up excited for my morning walk with my dogs. I feel proud—not because of a number on the scale, but because I kept a promise to myself and I'm living a healthier life that will give me the independence I want in old age."

To write your own one-year-from-now health statement, picture a year from now and ask yourself:

- What can my body do now that it previously couldn't?
- How am I now thinking about my health and how I'll maintain it?
- Besides the scale, what other signs will there be that I've changed?
- What am I most grateful for related to this new reality?

Now that I had a clear picture of what I want to see and feel a year from now, I need to **Lock in** on one clear goal.

L—Lock In On One Goal

Remember, it is important for The PLAN to WIN that you start with a single goal. You might add others later, but in the beginning, choose just one to plan out.

In this case, there were a lot of things I wanted to achieve in the coming year. To name a few, these included:

- Lose weight
- Train for a half-marathon
- Join a book club
- Write a book
- Learn how to knit

Given how I had pictured my life one year hence, I asked myself several questions, including:

- What single outcome would most impact my life?
- Which goal matters most to me or feels most urgent right now?
- Which goal helps my life align with my values?

It was immediately clear which one I had to go after—losing weight. I knew that losing weight would have the most significant impact on my life, including my ability to achieve other goals, such as training for a half-marathon and even starting a business. For both, I would need energy and stamina, which I didn't currently have. By working on dropping some pounds, I knew my overall health would begin to improve and make it possible for other activities I couldn't even consider at that moment.

I then wrote out my goal according to the SMART formula (Specific, Measurable, Achievable, Realistic, and Time-bound), which was:

- Specific: Lose seventy pounds
- Measurable: One to two pounds per week
- Achievable: Losing weight at that pace is doable, even

recommended

- Relevant: Getting healthier also makes other physical goals possible
- Time-bound: One year

"I will lose seventy pounds in the next twelve months by averaging one to two pounds per week through consistent calorie awareness, daily walking, and achievable food habit changes."

Focusing on a single target of seventy pounds in a year made decisions easier to make along the way. When I encountered a situation requiring a decision, I could ask myself, "Does my answer support losing weight or not?" I didn't always have to choose the path that supported my weight loss, of course, but it certainly kept that goal top of mind for me.

A—Analyze Your Starting Point

Before I could break down my goal and plan exactly how I was going to achieve it, I needed to assess where I was starting from. What habits did I have that would support or get in the way of my goal attainment?

Sometimes we don't know what we don't know. To figure that out, I started with a seven-day AWARE scan to make note of how I was living. How did I spend my time? What did I eat? What decisions was I making about when I ate and why?

The AWARE Scan: Losing Weight

A—Arrive in the Moment

My weekdays follow a structured routine centered around teaching. I don't struggle to wake up early for work, and I easily get around 9,500 steps a day. Although I eat lunch at work, it's often light and lacks vegetables, leaving me hungry, tired, and stressed by the time I get home. Most evenings, I shut down rather than make intentional choices, and I typically get six to seven hours of sleep per night.

W—Witness Without Judgment

When I imagine taking the next small step toward weight loss, I notice thoughts about lacking the energy to make better choices in the evening. Right before I go off-plan, the combination of hunger, fatigue, and stress feels automatic rather than deliberate. A neutral observer would say my routine supports movement and consistency, but it breaks down in terms of nutrition and recovery later in the day.

A—Allow What Is

My non-negotiable constraints include a full teaching schedule, early mornings, and limited energy in the evenings. I also impose constraints on myself by relying on convenience foods with few vegetables and expecting willpower to appear at night. On a hard day, the smallest action I can allow is adding vegetables to one meal or snack.

R—Root Yourself

Friends would describe me as disciplined and consistent, as shown by my early mornings and daily movement. My challenging habit loop is daytime depletion followed by feeling exhausted by dinner. Replacing that pattern with intentional vegetable intake earlier in the day supports steadier energy and better decisions at night.

E—Engage Mindfully

My five-minute version of progress is preparing or choosing one vegetable-forward meal or snack. "Done for today" means I included vegetables intentionally and avoided the evening shutdown. When resistance appears, I will pause rather than push, log the choice, and review patterns weekly to adjust.

As a companion analysis, I did a personal SWOT analysis, which stands for strengths, weaknesses, opportunities, and threats. Here is what I found:

SWOT Analysis: Weight Loss and Health Goal (Current Starting Point)

Strengths

- I enjoy walking and already have a strong movement foundation with a high daily step count.
- I have solid nutrition and exercise knowledge from my health coaching certification.
- My background in behavioral sciences gives me a clear understanding of what supports behavior change.
- I have a consistent early-morning routine that supports structure and reliability.

Weaknesses

- I tend to think in all-or-nothing terms, which at times can lead me to give up prematurely when conditions are not ideal.
- There's a gap between my knowledge and consistent action, particularly in the evenings.
- I often have light, low-vegetable meals earlier in the day, contributing to evening energy depletion.
- I have limited recovery and decision-making capacity at the end of long teaching days.

Opportunities

- I can meal prep at home, increasing access to vegetable-forward meals.
- I have support from a friend who also wants to begin a health journey, creating built-in accountability.
- I can leverage my existing daily movement without adding new demands.
- Tracking my patterns for better awareness allows for targeted, realistic adjustments.

Threats

- Test weeks, school events, and grading cycles significantly increase stress and reduce energy.
- Holiday travel and schedule disruptions interfere with routines.
- I risk reverting to shutdown behaviors during high-demand periods.
- I may over-rely on willpower during evenings rather than earlier, planned supports.

With the observations from these two analyses, I asked myself three questions to uncover how my current behaviors might be getting in the way of my goal. I asked:

1. When do I exhibit poor decision-making regarding food choices: in the morning, afternoon, evening, or on weekends?
2. What is the real cost of my habits in energy, mood, or longevity?
3. What patterns—fatigue cycles, stress eating, or all-or-nothing weeks—should I work around?

These two exercises made it clear that the main sabotaging pattern I needed to watch for was ordering food or going out for dinner when tired and stressed. But without these two assessments, I would not have known where I was starting from or recognized this particular behavior as a challenge.

Next, I needed to list everything I needed to do to reach my seventy-pound weight-loss goal.

N—Name the Elements

Naming the elements meant writing out everything I needed to do to reach my goal. These included things like a good scale to monitor how much I was eating, healthier snacks, supportive friends, new recipes to help me meet my goals, and easy access to my workout clothes.

W—Write It Out

From my long list, I identified five major categories (PERKS), which included people, environment, resources, knowledge, and skills. Each category represents a condition required to move from intention to consistent action.

People
- A friend who is also starting a health journey for accountability
- Supportive family or colleagues who respect health-focused routines

Environment
- Prepared vegetables available at home and ready to eat
- A predictable weekday routine that supports meals earlier in the day
- An evening environment that reduces decision fatigue

Resources
- Access to groceries and basic meal-prep tools at home
- Simple tracking method for meals, energy, and sleep
- Comfortable shoes and safe routes for daily walking

Knowledge
- How vegetable intake supports energy, satiety, and long-term weight management
- How stress, skipped nourishment, and sleep patterns affect evening decision-making

Skills
- Planning and preparing vegetable-forward meals that fit a busy teaching schedule
- Responding to hunger and stress without shutting down in

the evening

- Using small, repeatable habits instead of all-or-nothing thinking

It became clear that everything else was optional until these foundations were established.

Then, I asked myself three questions about how important each of these categories and changes were:

1. Which nutrition behavior, if mastered, would improve everything else?
2. What physical action gives me the highest return with the least effort?
3. What support—accountability, environment, or tools—has helped me before?

With those responses, I then took one non-negotiable from each category for my four non-negotiables in total:

1. A weekly meal prep plan/ half of every meal should be vegetables
2. A walking schedule
3. Tracking calories, portion sizes, and macros
4. Accountability weigh-ins every Saturday to track progress

At this point, I had a long list of tasks to complete to reach my goal, as well as a core list of four non-negotiables to keep top of mind. It was time to organize this information into my actual plan.

To start off strong, I divided the next twelve months into four quarters (ninety-one-day blocks/ thirteen weeks) of activity, with what seemed like realistic milestones at the end of each. Here is what each quarter plan initially looked like:

Quarter 1

- Walk thirty minutes each morning and ten minutes after school daily.
- Track calories and macros daily in the My Fitness Pal app.
- Meal prep four dinners and five lunches each week.

Milestone: Target weight loss of twenty-six pounds

Quarter 2
- Reach fourteen thousand steps daily.
- Track calories and macros daily in the My Fitness Pal app.
- Meal prep six dinners and five lunches each week.

Milestone: Target weight loss of twenty-two pounds

Quarter 3
- Walk fifteen thousand steps daily.
- Track calories and macros daily in My Fitness Pal app.
- Meal prep six dinners and five lunches each week.

Milestone: Target weight loss of eighteen pounds

Quarter 4
- Continue to walk fifteen thousand steps daily, but try to increase speed.
- Track calories and macros daily in My Fitness Pal app.
- Meal prep six dinners and five lunches each week.

Milestone: Target weight loss of the final fourteen pounds

With this initial framework, I then needed to plan out my first week, day by day, and make decisions to ensure my success. My first week was my last week of summer break, so I had one week to get my act together before I went back to work for the new school year.

Three questions I asked myself, so I could write out and order the steps of my first week, were:

1. What must happen on the weekends to make my weekday choices easier?
2. How will I track non-scale progress?
3. What small action will I take on low-energy days?

I plotted these action items on my physical calendar and set alarms on my phone as reminders. By being so specific, I really only had to follow the plan.

I—Implement the Plan

Of course, knowing what to do and actually doing it are two separate things.

Implementing the plan is just that—taking action, doing the things. Remember, this step is all about getting started, using your initial motivation as momentum to move forward, and surrounding yourself with all the things—the positive energy, people and quotes, etc.—that will support you in this phase and make you feel like you can do anything. Motivation won't get you to the finish line, but it will definitely get you started.

I played my favorite songs, found a mantra to recite every morning, called the people I knew who would offer support and encouragement, listened to my favorite motivational books and podcasts, and did anything else I could think of to keep my mind in the right direction. It took a while to notice the rewards of my efforts, so I call this step the "fake it till you make it" step.

I always reminded myself to just put one foot in front of the other and move forward.

It was inevitable that life would get in the way, and something would knock the wind out of my sails. But that is why the PLAN to WIN is the best system for REAL LIFE, because I planned for those challenges.

N—Navigate Challenges

I know that life is challenging, but that doesn't mean we can't still achieve our goals. We just need to have a plan to navigate those challenges.

I built a navigation strategy before I needed it, knowing that in the heat of the moment or under great stress, I wouldn't always be able to make smart choices. So, I thought them through in advance.

And knowing that you may struggle at times to take action, it's important to take steps to hold yourself accountable while making success easier.

My rule was not to "never break the plan," it was to "never go backwards."

Even on days when my progress faltered, I made sure I didn't revert to my all-or-nothing mindset. I practiced self-compassion, which was very difficult at first! But I also planned for what to do when unexpected challenges arose.

On a daily basis, I committed to:

- Forgiving myself if I couldn't do it fully; at least I would do it partially.
- Walking at least five minutes, even if I couldn't get my planned thirty-minute walk in the morning.

I also listed challenges I expected to surface and strategized how I would handle them. Here's what my list looked like:

- Challenge: Stress eating → Reset Strategy: Five-minute mindfulness meditation + vegetable snack first.
- Challenge: Poor sleep/ low energy → Reset Strategy: Walk anyway, even for a few minutes.
- Challenge: Weekend meals out → Reset Strategy: Resume normal meals immediately/ meal prep for the week.
- Challenge: Vacation disruption → Reset Strategy: Maintain steps + vegetable goal, use app to track as best as possible.

When I stumbled or did something that would not help me reach my goal, I referred back to a reset formula I created for myself, which included four actions I could take:

1. Taking a mindful pause without judgment
2. Saying aloud: "This is one moment, not the whole story"
3. Taking one tiny healthy action next
4. Reflecting on the weekly weigh-in session

I also created a toolbox of non-food relief options I could use:

- Hot shower
- Funny videos after my walk—not before
- Evening tea + blanket ritual with dogs
- Text or call my accountability buddy
- Yoga/stretch + music

What Actually Happened

My goal was to lose seventy pounds in a year. Each quarter, this is what I actually lost:

Quarter 1: At 3 months, I had lost a total of 29 pounds.

Quarter 2: At 6 months, I had lost a total of 43 pounds.

Quarter 3: At 9 months, I had lost a total of 50 pounds.

Quarter 4: At 12 months, I had lost a total of 57 pounds.

I definitely experienced an emotional drain when I hit my weight loss plateau, and I didn't lose seventy pounds. But learning to navigate social situations and focusing on progress, not perfection, really changed how I saw the end result. Removing the all-or-nothing thinking, the mindset shift that the Navigate Challenges step centers around, helped me realize that I didn't fail because I lost fifty-seven pounds. In fact, it is a huge success because I lost fifty-seven more pounds than I would have if I had done nothing. And I've successfully kept the weight off for more than a year.

I didn't just change my habits, I changed my identity and built a structure that made it easier to stick with the plan, even when things got tough.

If you want to lose some weight or adopt healthier habits but you're not yet convinced you can be successful, stop and ask yourself these three questions:

1. What has ended my past attempts, and how will I change that this time?
2. How will I tell the difference between needing rest and negotiating with myself to make bad choices?
3. What is your reset routine when you go off-plan?

If you can learn to approach your goals like I did—with clarity, structure, and self-respect—there is nothing in your life you cannot reshape.

Every meaningful transformation is simply:

Picture→ Lock In → Analyze→ Name→ Write→ Implement→ Navigate

That is how you win.

CHAPTER 10

USING THE PLAN TO WIN TO WRITE A BOOK

Chapter Objective: By the end of this chapter, you will be able to identify the steps I took to complete The PLAN to WIN book in one year while working full-time. You will see how I applied my insights on structuring learning and motivating students to write The PLAN to WIN, which helps adults achieve their goals.

What This Case Study Shows:
- You can write a successful book by first defining its purpose, audience, and promise.
- Creating a timeline with measurable checkpoints will help you complete your book within a specific timeframe.
- Writer's block is just an excuse—keep making progress by writing something, even if it's just a few words, every day.

- Knowing when to consider your book finished is crucial.

A Jenkins Group survey published in the *New York Times*[1] reported in 2002 that 81 percent of Americans want to write a book. That's not surprising, since so many people believe they have a story to tell. It's common knowledge in the writing community that only 3 percent of aspiring authors ever finish their manuscript, and 0.6 percent ever get their book published, though finding the original source of that data has proven challenging. It looks like Copper Mountain Books[2] did the math. However, despite the odds, in 2024 alone, close to one million books were published in the US—proof that some people do figure out how to turn their ideas into books. But that is still fewer than one-third of 1 percent of Americans who publish a book in a given year.

The takeaway here is that a lot of people want to write a book, but only three out of every thousand actually get it done. The ones who are successful often have a clear idea from the outset and a plan that helps them keep making progress even when motivation starts to wane. Other reasons books don't get written are:

- The concept keeps changing.
- Writing happens only when inspiration strikes.
- Endless editing prevents the draft from ever being finished.
- There's no clear vision of what "done" looks like.

Yes, you need a solid idea for a book and fifty to eighty thousand words of content to fill the pages, but most of all, you need a process to follow.

That's exactly what The PLAN to WIN provides—a step-by-step roadmap. Having used it for that exact purpose, I'm confident it can work for you.

As you can tell, I love setting and achieving goals. So, writing a how-to book on planning for goal achievement using the PLAN to WIN framework was exactly what I needed to do. You can write a book, too, using this system. Here's how to get started.

P—Picture Your Success

The first step is to write a vivid, present-tense description of the life you picture once your manuscript is finished in a year. What ideas do you have that you want to write about? Who is it for? When will you finish it? How will its publication change your life?

Picture it and write down what success looks like for you when you finish writing your book.

My own description of my success was a picture of me at a party, with someone asking me what I had done since they last saw me. Here is my imagined response that describes the picture of my success:

"This year, I realized that, as a 51-year-old Advanced Placement (AP) US History teacher, I have been teaching students how to organize projects and set goals for decades. So, I wrote a book that shows adults how to apply my classroom-tested planning strategies to achieving their career and personal goals. The book is fifty thousand words and is being edited for publication."

In that statement, you probably see and feel the pride I expected to feel after completing my book—the pride of being someone who turned my experience into tools that help others succeed. It was a significant accomplishment, partly because I knew by then that I would have clearly articulated my framework, shared it with my inner circle, and kicked off an entirely new chapter of my life as an author.

L—Lock In On One Goal

Wanting to be a published author and wanting to write a book are actually two different goals. Crafting an entire manuscript is a huge task, but having it produced and released as an official title is something else. Before I could proceed, I had to be clear about what I expected to accomplish in a year.

My goal became writing a book. The additional steps that follow are future steps. I wrote:

"I will complete, edit, and publish a full fifty-thousand-word manuscript of my planning for goal-achievement book within twelve months."

You'll see that the goal is SMART:

- Specific: A complete, edited, and published manuscript
- Measurable: Fifty thousand words
- Achievable: Given the timetable for the publishing piece of the process, I zeroed in on what I could do in twelve months
- Relevant: Not about building a brand but about the writing process itself
- Time-bound: One year

A—Analyze Your Starting Point

The AWARE Scan: Writing a First Book

A—Arrive in the Moment

I aim to write a fifty-thousand-word manuscript in twelve months, with one to two hours available most weekdays and longer blocks on weekends. I have a quiet home office and do my best writing in the morning. Although I have decades of experience creating structured written content, I still identify more as a teacher than an author.

W—Witness Without Judgment

When I imagine drafting, I quickly think about whether my writing is "good enough." Right before I procrastinate, I notice the urge to reread, revise, or reorganize rather than move forward. A neutral observer would say I plan and outline well, but I slow down when it's time to draft.

A—Allow What Is

My non-negotiable constraints are time available during grading seasons, limited daily writing windows, and mental fatigue after teaching. I also impose constraints on myself by overthinking and believing that clarity must come before writing. On a difficult day, the smallest action I can take is to write for ten minutes without editing.

R—Root Yourself

Friends and colleagues would describe me as a clear thinker, strong communicator, and skilled teacher. My challenging habit loop is drafting → self-criticism → overediting → stalled progress. Replacing that loop with drafting → stopping on purpose → returning fresh supports momentum and confidence.

E—Engage Mindfully

My five-minute version of progress is opening the document and writing one paragraph forward. "Done for today" means I added new words without revising old ones. When resistance appears, I will pause, remind myself that drafts are allowed to be messy, log my word count, and review progress weekly to adjust.

I then conducted a personal SWOT analysis to spot where I might run into trouble during the writing process.

SWOT Analysis: First-Time Book Writing Project

Strengths
- A strong writing voice shaped by over twenty-six years of teaching and curriculum design
- Deep experience structuring complex ideas into clear, teachable frameworks
- A large informal audience of former students and colleagues
- Consistent access to a quiet workspace and productive morning energy

Weaknesses
- No prior experience writing or publishing a book

- A tendency to overthink and overedit during the drafting phase
- An emerging author identity; I still primarily self-identify as a teacher
- The risk of slowing momentum by seeking clarity too early

Opportunities
- Growing public interest in cognitive behavioral psychology, planning, and behavior change
- The ability to leverage teaching expertise to differentiate the book's structure and clarity
- Financial resources available for a book coach or external accountability
- An existing professional network that can later support early readers and promotion

Threats
- Grading seasons and school demands that reduce writing capacity
- Perfectionism can delay completion
- Competing priorities during high-stress periods of the academic year
- The risk of burnout if writing expectations exceeds realistic energy limits

This assessment helped me avoid overplanning and to create a realistic writing schedule by noting my available time and my normal energy cycles. Understanding these realities helped me in the later step of writing it out, creating a realistic instead of an idealistic plan.

N—Name the Elements

Naming the elements involved identifying everything I had and would need to reach my goal, including finding a book coach, enlisting the support of my family and friends, researching a little online about writing books to find the best courses and books I could use for support, and outlining my system clearly.

The three elements I named that I would need to stay on course included:

1. A functional outline with a table of contents and chapter summaries.
2. At least four weekly writing sessions to make progress.
3. Avoiding major editing until the first seven chapters of the draft were complete.

W—Write It Out

Before writing the steps, I needed to organize all the elements into my PERKS (people, environment, resources, knowledge, skills).

People
- A book coach serving as an accountability partner
- Supportive family and friends who can act as alpha readers
- A developmental editor to review chapters one through seven once complete

Environment
- A dedicated home office for writing
- A protected two-hour daily writing block to stay focused

Resources
- A book coach for guidance
- Online courses on book writing

Knowledge
- Structuring a nonfiction argument

- Presenting my classroom-tested planning framework for adults

Skills
- Writing long-form content effectively
- Separating drafting from editing stages

To reach my twelve-month goal, I divided my project into four ninety-day cycles or quarters. I worked backwards from my goal and created these milestones:

Quarter 1—Extract and Organize Ideas
- Define the book's promise and identify my target reader.
- Create a draft outline and table of contents.
- Write the first chapter.

Milestone: Complete the chapter outline.

Quarter 2—Draft Core Concepts
- Write fifteen hundred to two thousand words weekly.
- Draft chapters one through seven without editing.

Milestone: Reach forty thousand words.

Quarter 3—Revise System and Draft Application Chapters
- Write application chapters using my own examples.
- Maintain my writing pace.
- Share the draft with three alpha readers, then revise the system presentation based on feedback.

Milestone: Complete the first draft at fifty thousand words.

Quarter 4—Read, Revise, and Publish
- Prepare a revised manuscript for professional review and make revisions.
- Hire a cover designer and an interior formatter.

- Register for LCCN and ISBN.
- Set up accounts for uploading the finished book.

Milestone: Prepare the book for publication.

With this initial framework completed, I planned out my first week, day by day, and made decisions to ensure my success. I plotted these action items on my physical calendar and set alarms on my phone as reminders. Because I was so specific, I only had to follow the plan.

I—Implement the Plan

Understanding the pace at which I needed to work to meet this goal, I began working on my book on the following schedule:

- Daily Writing Block: 5:00 am–7:00 am in my home office, before my morning walk.
- Daily Micro-Commitment: If I can't write for a full two hours for any reason, I will write at least one paragraph or voice-dictate my ideas.
- Weekly Book Coaching Sessions: Clarify ideas, discuss structure challenges, and accountability coach for progress.
- Weekly Log: Track word count and quality.

My big rule: If I miss a writing day, I must get back on track within twenty-four hours, even if for just twenty minutes.

Consistency, not intensity, leads to success.

N—Navigate Challenges

As always, it's necessary to be prepared for unexpected disruptions that can hinder progress. The disruptions I faced were:

- Tests and end-of-term grading in my day job
- Family and friend obligations
- Self-doubt: "Who am I to write this?"

Navigation Strategies:

- During busy times, switch to outlining, researching, or collecting ideas.
- When motivation drops, reread my "Year-End Vision."
- Have a weekly accountability check-in with a book coach, regardless of progress.

Plan B Work Options (When things don't go as planned):

- Dictate ideas into my phone.
- Add bullet points to chapter outlines to continue adding content.

By having these fallback activities, I ensured that even if writing slowed down, it wouldn't stop completely.

There were disruptions along the way, but they didn't derail me. I kept working, making steady progress by doing what I could when I had the time, even if it meant adding notes instead of writing straight away. I kept track of my word count targets to monitor my progress against my original plan.

This method is similar to what I do as a teacher to help my students tackle complex projects. Breaking larger goals into smaller chunks lets you focus on the next thing without getting overwhelmed by the bigger picture. When applied to adult life and personal dreams, it turns "thinking about writing a book" into "finishing one."

What Actually Happened

The year unfolded as planned, not because everything was easy, but because the structure could handle real life.

Quarter 1: I focused on thinking, not writing. I defined the book's purpose, identified my reader, and shaped the core promise of the PLAN to WIN framework. This quarter was for outlining, researching, and organizing my ideas. By the end, I had a clear structure that supported steady writing without constant rethinking.

Quarter 2: I shifted from planning to writing. This was the toughest phase mentally. I had to write imperfectly and resist the urge to revise. I treated writing like a job, showing up daily, and by the end, I had a substantial draft. It wasn't polished, but it was real, and that made it feel different.

Quarter 3: I moved from creating content to refining it. I tested the framework by reviewing chapters with fresh eyes and enlisted the assistance of professional editors and beta readers for feedback. I implemented feedback, clarified explanations, and strengthened examples. My goal wasn't perfection, but clarity, usefulness, and staying true to my system.

Quarter 4: I focused on getting the book out. Publishing tasks, such as formatting and cover design, replaced daily writing. The work was more logistical than creative, but the same system applied. Since the manuscript was complete, these steps felt manageable. By the end of the year, the book was finished and published.

What made this possible wasn't discipline or inspiration. It was the decision to treat writing as a process, not a test of motivation. Each quarter had a clear goal, each phase built on the last, and I could see progress even when my energy was low. That's the power of the PLAN to WIN system: it turns a big goal into a series of achievable tasks—and helps you follow through.

Every meaningful transformation is simply:

Picture → Lock In → Analyze → Name → Write → Implement → Navigate

That is how you win.

Information doesn't change people. Experiences do.
—Julie Dirksen

CHAPTER 11

USING THE PLAN TO WIN TO CREATE AN ONLINE COURSE

Chapter Objective: By the end of this chapter, you will be able to identify the key components involved in turning your subject matter expertise into an online course using the PLAN to WIN framework and see how intentional structure and sequencing support learner application of a system.

What This Case Study Shows:
- How to convert your expertise into a course outline.
- Creating a weekly rhythm for steady progress.
- Designing a sequenced module plan.
- Defining the transformational outcome students will achieve.

After finishing writing the PLAN to WIN book, I decided to

develop a course based on the framework to help readers and other users apply the system.

The global online education market is growing at about 8 percent per year and is expected to reach $279.3 billion by 2029, according to Statista.[1] In 2025, the US segment of that market is expected to generate just under $100 billion.

The opportunity here is huge and worth exploring.

People all over the world are turning their expertise and interests into online courses to generate passive income. If you have specialized knowledge or experience, or a unique set of skills that you know will help others, you may want to consider creating a course.

This chapter will show you how to use the PLAN to WIN system to design your own course and bring it to life so that you can share your knowledge with the world.

Here is how I converted my book into a multi-module course.

P—Picture Your Success

The start of any goal-setting session involves visualizing what success looks like for you. When creating a course, though, your attention turns to your students. So, you need to ask yourself: *What do I want my students to know or be able to do by the time they finish this course?*

Then, write out a description of what you envision when the course is complete. This is what I envisioned for my PLAN to WIN course:

"My new online course has launched, and I've enrolled twenty-five new students in my first cohort. I've built an email list of at least a hundred people interested in learning more about my course and who are potential future students. I know that when a person finishes this course, they will have an actionable PLAN to WIN, and I feel proud of what I've designed purely based on my own knowledge and experience."

Once I determined this, I needed to get specific about how I was going to get started in creating my course.

L—Lock In On One Goal

When I finished the PLAN to WIN book, I knew that the next logical step would be to create a course for people who wanted to see how it was done. That way, they would have experiential knowledge and know how to apply what they learned in the book.

I then wrote out my goal for my course according to the SMART formula, which was:

"I will design and launch a course about planning for goal achievement based on the PLAN to WIN framework to go live by October 2026 on an online teaching platform."

You'll see that the goal is also SMART:

- Specific: Design a course about planning
- Measurable: Launch by a specific date
- Achievable: Since the course is based on the book's framework, it essentially involves converting existing materials into a new format.
- Relevant: Helping expand the impact of the book
- Time-bound: Live by October 2026

A—Analyze Your Starting Point

It's always a good idea to know where you're starting from when you decide to do something you've never done before. In this case, I have extensive experience in the teaching world, but aside from a brief stint online during the pandemic, I have no online teaching experience. It is very different to teach adults asynchronously in an online course, but the elements of good course design will still be the same. As I always recommend when planning, I decided to do an AWARE scan to analyze my starting point.

AWARE Scan: Creating and Launching an Online Course

A—Arrive in the Moment

I have a clear plan and will launch an online course within twelve months, despite having no prior experience in creating a course for an online space. I can draw on decades of curriculum development and teaching, as well as my completed book, *The PLAN to WIN*, and extensive notes, readings, and in-person course materials. As a teacher at heart, I already possess most of the necessary skills and content.

W—Witness Without Judgment

When I think about turning my book into an online course, I worry about the differences between online and classroom learning. I feel impatient and uncertain about technology and being on camera. A neutral observer would say I'm confident in my content and structure, but hesitant about the delivery format and visibility.

A—Allow What Is

I face non-negotiable constraints like my full-time teaching job, limited weekly bandwidth, and a learning curve with online platforms. My self-imposed constraints include fearing being on camera and believing the course must immediately compete with highly polished programs. On tough days, the smallest action I can take is to outline one lesson or organize existing material.

R—Root Yourself

Colleagues see me as an expert planner and effective educator. My challenging habit loop is getting excited, then impatient, and finally frustrated with slow progress. Replacing that loop with steady, milestone-based planning helps me stay grounded and consistent.

E—Engage Mindfully

My five-minute progress is to review my book and tag content for course lessons. "Done for today" means I clarified one decision about structure, format, or flow. When resistance appears, I'll pause, remind myself that clarity comes from building, log the action, and review progress weekly to adjust.

After the AWARE scan, I completed a SWOT analysis on myself.

SWOT Analysis: First-Time Online Course Creation

Strengths

- I authored *The PLAN to WIN*, providing a solid content foundation.
- I have over twenty-six years of planning and teaching experience.
- I'm deeply familiar with curriculum structure, sequencing, and learning objectives.
- I enjoy the planning process itself.

Weaknesses

- I have no prior experience designing or launching an online course.
- I have time limitations due to my full-time teaching role.
- I can get impatient with slow or iterative progress.
- I dislike being on camera.

Opportunities

- I have extensive existing content from books, notes, readings, and in-person teaching.
- I have a large support network of teachers and friends who align with the course topic.
- I can design a course grounded in real-world application rather than theory.
- I selected an online platform that provides a built-in structure and tools.

Threats

- The online course market is highly saturated.
- I might compare my course to polished, high-budget ones.
- I risk overbuilding or overcomplicating the course before launch.
- I might burn out if my expectations exceed my realistic capacity.

Understanding where I am starting from gives me confidence to move forward with the plan, knowing that progress is better than perfection.

N—Name the Elements

Naming the elements required for the course means listing every step needed to design and build an online course. I made my list by thinking through the course design process from start to finish.

This list included:

- Objectives for each module that would align with the chapters of the book
- Outlines for each module
    - Learning activities that complete the objectives and are engaging
    - Materials I would need to create to accompany the various modules
        - Guiding questions
        - Templates and handouts
- Script outline
- Technology

Naming the steps involved in creating a course starts with identifying the core modules, then breaking down each module to ensure you convey what your learner needs before proceeding to the next module.

W—Write It Out

Referring to my long list of steps to create a course, I first put them into categories (PERKS: people, environment, resources, knowledge, skills), then ordered them chronologically and grouped them by quarter, setting milestones along the way. Remember, milestones are important because they help confirm you've made solid progress, even when it may not feel that way day to day.

My five categories included:

People

- An experienced reviewer (such as an educator, planner, or course mentor) to review the scope and sequencing
- A small group of trusted teachers or planners who agreed to test the course and provide early feedback on clarity and pacing
- Optional technical support for setting up and troubleshooting the platform

Environment

- A dedicated, quiet workspace for course design and development
- Weekly blocks for course building scheduled around full-time teaching responsibilities
- A low-interruption environment that allows for deep planning and content creation

Resources

- The PLAN to WIN book as the main resource
- Existing lesson plans, in-person course notes, and planning frameworks
- A selected online course platform to guide decisions and define constraints
- Basic tools for content creation (laptop, microphone, simple recording software)

Knowledge

- How to turn book content into teachable, outcome-driven modules
- Adult learning principles and behavior change knowledge (developed through past teaching experience)
- A clear understanding of what makes a minimum viable course for a first launch

Skills

- Breaking down complex ideas into modules, lessons, and activities
- Writing clear learning objectives that align with outcomes
- Designing activities that lead to action, not just understanding
- Managing impatience, avoiding overbuilding, and finishing planned work

Quarter 1

- Define course objectives
- Outline course content overview
- Outline each individual module

Milestone: A completed course outline

Quarter 2

- Design learning activities for each module
- Create slides for each module
- Design and create all accompanying materials

Milestone: Course design and materials complete

Quarter 3

- Write scripts for each module
- Practice and time scripts for each module
- Record all videos for all modules

Milestone: Course recordings completed

Quarter 4
- Create and upload a sales page to the website
- Create and upload sales materials and messages for the launch
- Upload course videos and materials to the teaching platform
- Beta run the course to catch errors
- Announce course availability

Milestone: Launch fully designed course

Breaking a twelve-month-long goal into quarters, or whatever timeframe makes sense to you, allows you to check in with yourself and notice all that you've accomplished along the way at regular intervals throughout your plan.

With this initial framework completed, I planned out my first week, day by day, and made decisions to ensure my success. I plotted these action items on my physical calendar and set alarms on my phone as reminders. By being so specific, I really only had to follow the plan.

I—Implement the Plan

Now that I laid out the plan, in theory, it should be easy to execute. Only, it rarely is. Planning and doing are very different activities.

In this case, implementing involves designing the course curriculum and then making it available on the teaching platform I chose. It involves converting my book into a step-by-step process that students can access online.

Once the course was set up, it was time to start promoting it. Essentially, that involved letting people who might be interested know that they could register and take it. I did that through email campaigns, course landing pages, and blog posts announcing the course.

This was the step when everything came together.

N—Navigate Challenges

Of course, despite my best efforts, things came up that I didn't expect.

When that happened, I stayed true to making at least some progress daily. Some of my unexpected challenges included:

- Catching the flu and being unable to finish a module when I expected to.
- Forgetting to save my files at one point and having to start over.
- Deciding to add more content to make the course even easier to follow.
- Getting a new puppy, which needed constant supervision for the first few months.

While these kind of scenarios can be frustrating and inconvenient, they are all completely solvable. You can figure out a workaround.

What Actually Happened

Quarter 1: Using my completed book, the course objectives were defined, and each module was outlined.

Quarter 2: Learning activities were designed and created alongside the slides for each module. All materials were complete.

Quarter 3: Script outlines were written instead of full scripts to ensure flexibility and a natural pace. This decision came after writing a full script and rehearsing it. I felt it sounded too robotic and decided to use bullet points instead of a full script. Recording was started but not completed at this stage.

Quarter 4: Sales page was created and added to the website. All materials for the sales funnel were created and linked. Video recordings were completed, edited, and uploaded to the platform. A beta test was run, and a few errors were corrected before launching the course.

Every meaningful transformation is simply:

Picture→ Lock In → Analyze → Name → Write → Implement → Navigate

That is how you win.

(If you'd like to join the waitlist for my next course launch, go to www.springhempsey.com)

Systems create freedom.
—James Clear

EPILOGUE

As I started writing this book, I realized that this system isn't just about teaching a new-and-improved approach to AP US History, which is where this whole process started. It's about creating success in a complex environment. The same issues that hinder students—overload, unclear priorities, inconsistent execution, and decision fatigue—also hold adults back from achieving their goals.

PLAN to WIN was designed to manage complexity, reduce obstacles, and build momentum when the stakes are high and errors are costly. What works in a classroom with real limits also applies to any situation requiring effort, careful planning, and consistent follow-through.

Lisa's Journey

If you see yourself in Lisa, the aspiring caterer, you're not alone. Many driven people feel stuck, not because they lack ideas or motivation but when goals are vague and set for "someday," they often get sidelined by urgent tasks. Lisa's story shows the power of treating goals as plans to design, not just wishes. With a solid system, you can stay on track, even when motivation wanes.

You've now learned the process of planning how to achieve a

goal, which you can apply to nearly any situation you encounter. Want to explore switching careers, look ahead to retirement, set up a nonprofit organization, or learn to surf? You now have the know-how to design a plan to do exactly that.

Keep in mind that every day you follow your plan, you are one step closer to achieving your goal. It may not seem like you're making much progress early on, but the more you consistently check off the tasks on your daily to-do list, the closer you are to success. It's like a snowball rolling downhill—it picks up speed and more snow the farther it rolls.

That's not to say that all the days you've put in the time and energy weren't important—they are! In fact, each day that you execute your plan, you've won, because you are one step closer to achieving your ultimate goal. Every time you complete any part of the task you set yourself up for that day, you are, in fact, prepping yourself for that goal.

Research shows that people who follow structured, step-by-step plans achieve more goals. Plans help reduce cognitive load and decision fatigue; they allow you to pursue your goal even when you're not particularly motivated, and they keep you on track simply by being there. Taking the time to think through what, exactly, you have to do to reach your goal makes you so much more likely to get there.

You started this book with a dream. Now you have the PLAN to WIN. The only question left is: What will this plan make possible for you?

I can't wait to learn about what you accomplish!

ACKNOWLEDGEMENTS

The biggest THANK YOU goes to William and Katie for believing in this idea from the very beginning and for your steady encouragement throughout the journey.

I am also deeply grateful to those who read early drafts of this manuscript, helped me edit and prepare the book for publication, and generously shared their knowledge, insights, feedback, and encouragement: Marcia Turner, Connie Medina, Brianna McCabe, Lenora Henson, Jenn DePaula, and Elizabeth Lyons—thank you for your time, thoughtfulness, and expertise. This book is stronger because of your contributions.

The following books are works I have read and learned from. They informed my knowledge and understanding, which ultimately contributed to the development of the principles and steps presented in this book. They are excellent resources for readers who wish to explore these ideas more deeply.

Clear, James. *Atomic Habits: An Easy & Proven Way to Build Good Habits & Break Bad Ones*. Avery, 2018.

Davis, Susan David. *Emotional Agility: Get Unstuck, Embrace Change, and Thrive in Work and Life*. Avery, 2016.

Dirksen, Julie. *Design for How People Learn*. 2nd ed. New Riders, 2016.

Duhigg, Charles. *The Power of Habit: Why We Do What We Do in Life and Business*. Random House, 2012.

Dweck, Carol S. *Mindset: The New Psychology of Success*. Ballantine Books, 2006.

Harris, Dan. *10% Happier: How I Tamed the Voice in My Head, Reduced Stress Without Losing My Edge, and Found Self-Help That Actually Works*. HarperCollins, 2014.

Keller, Gary, and Jay Papasan. *The ONE Thing: The Surprisingly Simple Truth Behind Extraordinary Results*. Bard Press, 2013.

Milkman, Katy. *How to Change: The Science of Getting from Where You Are to Where You Want to Be*. Portfolio, 2021.

McGonigal, Kelly. *The Willpower Instinct: How Self-Control Works, Why It Matters, and What You Can Do to Get More of It*. Avery, 2011.

Tracy, Brian. *Eat That Frog!: 21 Great Ways to Stop Procrastinating and Get More Done in Less Time*. 3rd ed. Berrett-Koehler Publishers, 2017.

Introduction

1. Brian Tracy, *Eat That Frog!: 21 Great Ways to Stop Procrastinating and Get More Done in Less Time* (Berrett-Koehler Publishers, 2017).

Chapter 1: P—Picture Your Success

1. Alan, Richardson, (1967). "Mental Practice: A Review and Discussion Part I." *Research Quarterly: American Association for Health, Physical Education and Recreation*, 38, no.1 (1967): 95–107.

2. Tim Blankert and Melvyn R.W. Hamstra, "Imagining Success: Multiple Achievement Goals and the Effectiveness of Imagery," *Basic and Applied Social Psychology* 39, no. 1 (2017): 60–67, https://doi.org/10.1080/01973533.2016.1255947.

3. *Reference for Business,* "Martha Stewart," accessed month, date, year, https://www.referenceforbusiness.com/biography/S-Z/Stewart-Martha-1941.html.

Chapter 2: L—Lock In On One Goal

1. Amy Lifson, "Reading Laura Ingalls Wilder Is Not the Same When You're a Parent," Humanities 35, no. 4, (July/August 2014), https://www.neh.gov/humanities/2014/julyaugust/feature/reading-laura-ingalls-wilder-not-the-same-when-youre-parent.

2. Gary W. Keller and Jay Papasan, The ONE Thing: The Surprisingly Simple Truth Behind Extraordinary Results (Bard Press, 2013).

3. Joshua S. Rubinstein, David E. Meyer, and Jeffrey E. Evans, "Executive Control of Cognitive Processes in Task Switching." *Journal of Experimental Psychology: Human Perception and Performance*, 27, no. 4 (2001): 763–797.

4. James Clear, *Atomic Habits: An Easy & Proven Way to Build Good Habits & Break Bad Ones*. Avery (Penguin Random House, 2018).

5. *WWD: Women's Wear Daily*, "How Vera Wang Went from Ice Skater to the A-List Crowd's Top Bridal Designer," November 3, 2023, https://wwd.com/pop-culture/celebrity-news/feature/vera-wang-history-1235909839/.

6. *Biography*, "Vera Wang," updated May 13, 2024, https://www.biography.com/history-culture/vera-wang.

7. Laurel Deppen, "Vera Wang Sells Namesake Brand to WHP Global," *Fashion Dive*, December 16, 2024, https://www.fashiondive.com/news/vera-wang-sells-to-whp-global/735632/.

8. "Driver Improvement," AAA, accessed month, date, year, https://www.ace.aaa.com/automotive/driver-education/driver-improvement.html.; "What is Defensive Driving? Driver Safety Course," AARP, accessed month, date, year, https://www.aarpdriversafety.org/california-defensive-driving-course.

Chapter 3: A—Analyze your Starting Point

1. Julia Child and Alex Prud'homme, *My Life in France* (Alfred A. Knopf, 2006).

2. Taylor Barnes, "New Year's Resolutions: Why Do We Give up on Them So Quickly?" *News* (Baylor College of Medicine), January 11, 2024, https://www.bcm.edu/news/new-years-resolutions-why-do-we-give-up-on-them-so-quickly.

3. Richard Batts, "Why Most New Year's Resolutions Fail," *Lead Read Today* (Blog, Fischer College of Business, The Ohio State University), February 2, 2023,https://fisher.osu.edu/blogs/leadreadtoday/why-most-new-years-resolutions-fail.

4. *Psychology Today,* "Hedonic Treadmill," accessed month, date, year, https://www.psychologytoday.com/us/basics/hedonic-treadmill.

5. Angel E. Navidad, "Stanford Marshmallow Test Experiment," *Simply Psychology*, updated September 7, 2023, https://www.simplypsychology.org/marshmallow-test.html.

Chapter 4: N—Name the Elements

1. Matthew Bailey, "The Home Depot," *New Georgia Encyclopedia*, updated June 8, 2017, https://www.georgiaencyclopedia.org/articles/business-economy/the-home-depot/.

2. Bailey, "The Home Depot," 2017.

3. Ann Schmidt, "How Arthur Blank, Bernie Marcus, Co-Founded Home Depot After Being Fired, *FOXBusiness,* August 2, 2020, https://www.foxbusiness.com/money/arthur-blank-bernie-marcus-home-depot-winning-formula.

4. Chris Yogerst, "How Stan Lee Became the Man Behind Marvel," *Los Angeles Review of Books,* April 21, 2018, https://lareviewofbooks.org/article/how-stan-lee-became-the-man-behind-marvel/.

5. Yogerst, "Stan Lee," 2018.

Chapter 5: W—Write It Out

1. Bill Walsh, "A Method for Game Planning," *West Coast Offence*, accessed, month, date, year, http://www.west-coastoffense.com/bill%20walsh%20method%20for%20game%20planning.htm.

2. Yanliu Huang, Zhen Yang, and Vicki G. Morwitz, "How Using a Paper versus Mobile Calendar Influences Everyday Planning and Plan Fulfillment," *Journal of Consumer Psychology* 33 (2023): 115–122. https://doi.org/10.1002/jcpy.1297.

3. Gail Matthews, "The Impact of Commitment, Accountability, and Written Goals on Goal Achievement," Psychology Faculty Conference Presentations, Dominican University of California, 2007, https://scholar.dominican.edu/cgi/viewcontent.cgi?article=1002&context=psychology-faculty-conference-presentations.

4. Ran Kivetz, Oleg Urminsky, and Yuhuang Zheng, "The Goal-Gradient Hypothesis Resurrected: Purchase

Acceleration, Illusionary Goal Progress, and Customer Retention, *Journal of Marketing Research* 43 (February 2006): 39–58. https://home.uchicago.edu/ourminsky/Goal-Gradient_Illusionary_Goal_Progress.pdf.

5. F.R. (Ruud) Van der Weel and Audrey L. H. Van der Meer, "Handwriting but Not Typewriting Leads to Widespread Brain Connectivity: A High-Density EEG Study with Implications for the Classroom," *Frontiers in Psychology* 14 (January 2024) https://pmc.ncbi.nlm.nih.gov/articles/PMC10853352/.

6. J.R.R. Tolkien, *The Letters of J.R.R. Tolkien*, ed. Humphrey Carpenter with Christopher Tolkien (Houghton Mifflin Harcourt, 1981), 177.

Chapter 6: I—Implement the Plan
1. "The Construction of Disneyland," Designing Disney, accessed month, date, year, https://www.designingdisney.com/parks/disneyland-resort/construction-disneyland/.

2. "Mary Kay Launches Her Namesake Makeup Company," *This Day in History*, History, updated February 18, 2025, https://www.history.com/this-day-in-history/september-13/mary-kay-launches-namesake-makeup-company.

3. W.S. Strong, "Pink Cadillacs and Lucky 13: How Mary Kay Ash Built a Billion-Dollar Business," *Texas Standard,* June 27, 2018, https://www.texasstandard.org/stories/pink-cadillacs-and-lucky-13-how-mary-kay-ash-built-a-billion-dollar-business/.

4. Wendy Wood, Jeffrey M. Quinn, and Deborah A. Kashy, "Habits in Everyday Life: Thought, Emotion, and Action," *Journal of Personality and Social Psychology* 83, no. 6 (2002): 1281–1297.

Chapter 7: N—Navigate Challenges

1. "The 5 Failures of Susan Wojcicki and How She Overcame Them," *pressfarm*, October 2, 2025, https://press.farm/5-failures-of-susan-wojcicki-how-she-overcame/.

2. "Susan Wojcicki," 2025.

3. original endnote #35: about:blank

4. Daniel Lieberman, "Netflix CEO Reed Hastings Predicts 50% of TV Viewing from Web in Decade: UBS Confab," *Deadline*, December 6, 2011, https://deadline.com/2011/12/netflix-ceo-predicts-half-of-tv-viewing-on-web-in-10-years-ubs-confab-201717/.

5. Ken Favaro, "Netflix Wasn't All Wrong," *Strategy + Business*, April 2, 2012, https://www.strategy-business.com/article/cs00003.

6. "Former Netflix CEO, Reed Hastings' Guide for Successful Entrepreneurs," *pressfarm,* October 2, 2025, https://press.farm/founder-ceo-netflix-reed-hastings-definitive-startup-guide-successful-entrepreneurs/.

Chapter 8: Using the PLAN to WIN to Start a Business

1. Jeffrey M. Jones, "Desire to Be Own Boss Widely Held in US," *Gallup,* June 6, 2024, https://news.gallup.com/poll/645593/desire-own-boss-widely-held.aspx.

2. "New Advocacy Report Shows the Number of Small Businesses in the US Exceeds 36 Million," US Small Business Administration Office of Advocacy, June 30, 2025, https://advocacy.sba.gov/2025/06/30/new-advocacy-report-shows-the-number-of-small-businesses-in-the-u-s-exceeds-36-million/.

Chapter 9: Using the PLAN to WIN to Lose Weight

1. Megan Brenan, "43% of Americans Say They Are Overweight; 55% Want to Slim Down," *Gallup*. December 26, 2024, https://news.gallup.com/poll/654425/americans-say-overweight-slim-down.aspx.

2. "The New Year's Resolution Trap: Why 80% of Weight Loss Goals Fail," Lifestyle Medical Centers, December 20, 2024, https://lifestylemedicalcenters.com/why-weight-loss-new-years-resolutions-fail/.

Chapter 10: Using the PLAN to WIN to Write a Nonfiction Book

1. Joseph Epstein, "Thing You Have a Book in You? Think Again," Opinion, *New York Times,* September 28, 2002, https://www.nytimes.com/2002/09/28/opinion/think-you-have-a-book-in-you-think-again.html.

2. "The Swift Book Method Comparison Chart," Copper Mountain Books, accessed month, date, year, https://www.coppermountainbooks.com/.

Chapter 11: Using the PLAN to WIN to Create an Online Course

1. Market Insights, eCommerce, "Online Education Worldwide," *Statista*, accessed month, date, year,

https://www.statista.com/outlook/emo/online-educa-
tion/worldwide.

Spring Hempsey is a master planner and dedicated educator. She has a master's degree from the University of Miami and has taught over three thousand students in her career as a high school teacher.

In *The PLAN to WIN*, Spring uses her planning expertise to help people break free from feeling stuck and make meaningful progress toward their goals by planning for real life, not ideal life. She provides a step-by-step system with simple, actionable steps to make achieving goals a reality.

Spring lives in the suburbs of Los Angeles with her dogs. She enjoys reading, writing, watching TV, and going to the movies. She also likes hiking, doing jigsaw puzzles, and traveling. During her vacations, she loves exploring new places and has visited over eighty countries across all seven continents.

You can connect with Spring at www.springhempsey.com.